On the Santa Fe Trail

The End of the Trail, *a painting by Gerald Cassidy of the Santa Fe plaza when it was the end of the Santa Fe Trail (courtesy Museum of New Mexico, negative 6977)*

On the Santa Fe Trail

edited and with
an introduction by

Marc Simmons

 University Press of Kansas

Published by the University Press of Kansas (Lawrence, Kansas 66049), which was
organized by the Kansas Board of Regents and is operated and funded by Emporia
State University, Fort Hays State University, Kansas State University, Pittsburg State
University, the University of Kansas, and Wichita State University

Library of Congress Cataloging-in-Publication Data
On the Santa Fe Trail.
  Bibliography: p.
  1. Santa Fe Trail. 2. West (U.S.)—Description and travel. 3. Pioneers—West
(U.S.)—Diaries.
I. Simmons, Marc.
F786.06   1986   917.8'042   86-19001
ISBN 0-7006-0315-8
ISBN 0-7006-0316-6 (pbk.)

Printed in the United States of America
10 9 8 7 6 5 4

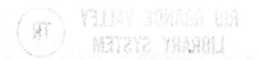

It is fitting
that this book be dedicated
to three stalwart Kansans
who have helped preserve the
memory of the old trail:
the late Amelia Betts of Baldwin City,
Ralph Hathaway of Chase,
and Paul Bentrup of Deerfield

Contents

List of Illustrations ix

Introduction 1

1. Report of Manuel Alvarez, 1842 6

2. Report on Winter Travel, 1852 11

3. Trail Letter by Michael Steck, 1852 18

4. James M. Fugate's Adventures, 1853 28

5. Narrative by Hezekiah Brake, 1858 37

6. David Kellogg's Diary, 1858 52

7. Henry Smith's Recollections, 1863 64

8. Ernestine Franke Huning's Diary, 1863 73

9. Reminiscences of George E. Vanderwalker, 1864 84

10. Major John C. McFerran's Report and Journal, 1865 96

11. Captain Charles Christy's Memoirs, 1867 106

12. José Librado Gurulé's Recollections, 1867 120

Appendix A. To Santa Fe via the Cimarron Cut-off 135

viii   Contents

Appendix B. To Santa Fe via the Bent's Fort Route   137

Recommended Readings   139

Index   141

List of Illustrations

The End of the Trail   frontispiece

Santa Fe Trail (map)   x

Courthouse Square, Independence, Missouri   2

Dr. Michael Steck   19

Pawnee Rock   33

A wagon train on the Santa Fe Trail   34

Hezekiah Brake   38

Round Mound   50

Freight wagons at Cow Creek Crossing   56

A Santa Fe Trail freight wagon   67

Franz Huning   74

Ernestine Franke Huning   76

George E. Vanderwalker   86

Plan of Fort Zarah   113

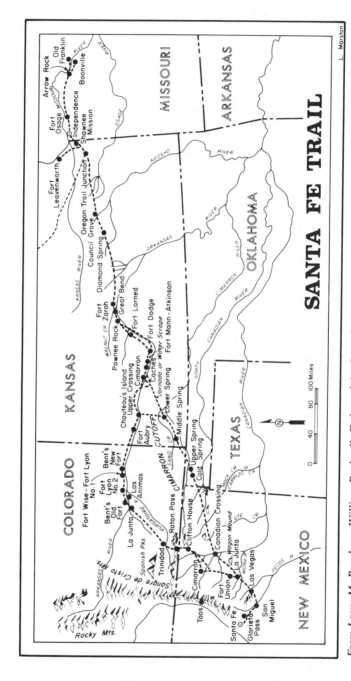

From Larry M. Beachum, William Bucknell: Father of the Santa Fe Trade (El Paso: Texas Western Press, 1982). Used with permission.

Introduction

When Missouri won statehood in 1821, its frontier residents had only a fuzzy idea of the great lands stretching westward toward the Pacific. Fur trappers and Indian traders had brought back tales of the prairie, the desert, and the mountains, but their descriptions corresponded with little that was familiar to pioneers raised in the woodlands of the East. Even more foreign were the stories of distant Santa Fe, capital of Spain's outpost province of New Mexico. Americans were not welcome there, and the few who had slipped across the international boundary for a bit of sightseeing or trade usually landed in a prison cell. Yet, upon being released and returning home, they spoke of the city as an alluring place and one that had ready markets, should Yankee merchants find some way to pierce the barriers that Spain had raised against commerce.

Actually, the Spanish colonists themselves resolved that problem, by casting off the yoke of the mother country, proclaiming independence for the new nation of Mexico (also in 1821), and opening the northern border to trade with the United States. William Becknell, a small-businessman from Franklin, Missouri, got a jump on competitors by starting for Santa Fe with a pack train in September, even before Mexico's independence had been fully confirmed. His arrival back in Franklin early in the following year, his mules loaded with rawhide bags of silver, signaled the completion of the first successful mercantile venture to New Mexico and the launching of the long and prosperous Santa Fe trade.

Some picture of that colorful and dramatic enterprise can be gathered from an editorial in a February, 1830, issue of the *Missouri Intelligencer,* the first newspaper established on the frontier west of St. Louis: "The inland trade between the United States and Mexico is increasing rapidly. This is perhaps one of the most curious species

1

Courthouse Square in Independence, Missouri, when it was the beginning of the Santa Fe Trail (from The United States Illustrated *[1853])*

---

of foreign intercourse which the ingenuity of American traders ever originated. The extent of country which the caravans traverse, the long journeys they have to make, the rivers and morasses to cross, the prairies, the forests and all but African deserts to penetrate, require the most steel-formed constitutions and the most energetic minds. The accounts of these inland expeditions remind one of the caravans of the East. The dangers which both encounter—the caravan of the East and that of the West—are equally numerous and equally alarming. Men of high chivalric and somewhat romantic natures are requisite for both.''[1]

In retrospect, the history of the Santa Fe Trail seems to be overlaid with the gloss of romance and chivalry. It is set off by heroic attitudes and picturesque adventures. And it has left a deep imprint on one region of the American West.

The trail crossed parts of five present-day states—Missouri, Kansas, Oklahoma, Colorado, and New Mexico—which, from the perspective of the overland trade, are forever bound in historical communion. The route began in Missouri and ended, after almost a

[1] Quoted by R. L. Duffus in *The Santa Fe Trail* (New York: Longmans, Green & Co., 1931), p. 108.

thousand miles, in New Mexico. But it was Kansas that claimed the largest share of the trail: from a beginning point at either Kansas City or Fort Leavenworth, it angled across the entire state, exiting over four hundred miles later in the southwestern corner. It would be no exaggeration to say that trade and travel on the Santa Fe Trail derived much of its special flavor from the Kansas experience and that, in turn, the presence of the trail went a long way toward shaping the early history of the state.

Many participants in this story, overlanders of various kinds, wrote down what they saw and learned on the way to Santa Fe. A number of these firsthand accounts have been published, particularly ones that are lengthy and detailed. One collection of shorter diaries, published in 1933 by Archer Butler Hulbert, was entitled *Southwest on the Turquoise Trail.*[2] This dealt only with the very earliest years, the period before 1825. Another contribution was made by Kate L. Gregg in *The Road to Santa Fe,* which printed the journals of George C. Sibley and others involved in the federal survey of the trail that got under way in 1825.[3] Plenty of room remains, however, for additional collections of brief documents whose publication can illuminate subsequent chapters of the trail's history.

With that purpose in mind, I have assembled here a dozen contemporary narratives and reports, which I offer to all who entertain an interest in the part of America's pioneering movement that flowed southwestward over the prairies to New Mexico. The time frame can be described as the Santa Fe Trail's middle years, the period from the 1840s to the latter 1860s, that is, the era just after New Mexico had passed into American hands. The authors, with the possible exception of United States Consul Manuel Alvarez, qualify as plain folk who, without quite intending to, got swept up in the westering adventure.

These persons had a variety of backgrounds and an assortment of reasons for traveling to Santa Fe. Among these writers were several teenagers, an army major, a government scout, a Spanish aristocrat, an Indian agent, a German immigrant lady, and a young New Mexican drover of the peon class. Through their eyes the

[2] Archer Butler Hulbert, ed., *Southwest on the Turquoise Trail* (Denver, Colo.: Denver Public Library, 1933).

[3] Kate L. Gregg, ed., *The Road to Santa Fe* (Albuquerque: University of New Mexico Press, 1952).

business of trailing is seen from different angles, and new perspectives are opened.

Throughout all the accounts, two persistent themes emerge: trail travel was filled with hardship, most of all in winter months; and the danger from Indian raiders was an abiding and terrifying one. One of the authors, James M. Fugate, seemed to be speaking to both points when he wrote of his 1853 caravan trip: "Kansas was then one vast wild plain, over which roving bands of hostile Indians were constantly cutting off emigrant and freight trains on their way to New Mexico and the Californias" (see document 4).

Readers will quickly observe the negative or, more forcefully stated, highly prejudicial view that the majority of these chroniclers held toward the Redmen. George E. Vanderwalker claimed that he would have preferred to have as a pet a rattlesnake with seventeen buttons on its tail, rather than an Indian. And Charles Christy condemned James Fenimore Cooper's novels for throwing a hero's halo over the heads of bloodthirsty savages. Before censuring such statements out of hand, it is best to remember that they were made in the context of the times by individuals who had come face to face with the brutality of frontier warfare. Acknowledging that fact will help us to achieve some measure of balance in understanding them.

Conflict with the Indians was confined mainly to the 1850s and the 1860s, the very years covered in this book. During that interval the army built Forts Larned, Dodge, Aubry, Lyons, and Union and Camp Nichols at trailside to protect a rising tide of traffic. Part of the increase came from military freighters who hurried to supply the new posts. By 1870 the hostilities had largely shifted away from the Santa Fe Trail, to remoter areas of the Great West, where the native peoples were making their last, futile stand. Thus, the final decade of the trail story was taken up, not with defense, but with the advance of the railroad.

As railroad track pushed relentlessly across Kansas, through southeastern Colorado, and over Raton Pass into New Mexico, the historic caravan route shriveled in length before it. On July 4, 1879, the rails reached Las Vegas, New Mexico, only sixty-five miles east of Santa Fe. During the next seven months, one freighting outfit—Otero, Seller & Company—continued to haul goods from the railhead over the last short strip of trail. But its services came to an end the following February, in 1880, as the first steam engine entered New Mexico's capital. The Santa Fe Trail had been extinguished, and it passed into the graveyard of history.

With the elapse of time, the chronicle of the trail has gathered about it a dreamlike quality, for within its pages can be found that curious mix of illusion and stark reality that characterized pioneering in the nineteenth-century West. Looking back at it now, the peril and misery that travelers knew fade from view, and what is left are the entrancing images of huge freight wagons, topped by canvas clouds, creaking under three-ton loads, as mighty ox teams lean into their yokes. And we are left, too, with specters of men and women, like those whose words appear in this book, who found in the journey to Santa Fe an opportunity to define themselves anew and an adventure so memorable that it would remain in the forepart of their minds to the end of their days.

Some of the narratives and reports that I present here are being published for the first time. The remainder appeared in obscure periodicals or in government documents printed either in the nineteenth or in the early twentieth century, where they have not been readily accessible to the general reader or even to the researcher. The source of each item is identified in the footnotes.

In the Appendixes can be seen a list of major trail sites as they were encountered, in succession, by travelers to Santa Fe. The names thereon will be found sprinkled through the narratives and reports. To further aid in establishing the location of principal sites, a reference map has been included.

In the preparation of this work, I gratefully acknowledge the assistance of Larry Jochims, Kansas State Historical Society, Topeka; Carol Joiner, Zimmerman Library, University of New Mexico, Albuquerque; Catherine Engle, Colorado Historical Society, Denver; Eleanor Gehres, Denver Public Library; Janet Lecompte, Colorado Springs; Jacqueline Meketa, Corrales, New Mexico; Lee Myres, Las Cruces, New Mexico; and my typist, Susie Henderson, Cerrillos, New Mexico.

1. Report of Manuel Alvarez, 1842

One of the most interesting persons associated with the early Santa Fe trade was the distinguished and cultured merchant Don Manuel Alvarez. In 1818, at the age of twenty-four, he left his native Spain and immigrated to Mexico. Five years later he moved to New York, and the next year, 1824, found him in Missouri, engaged in merchandising. Apparently a desire to resume residence in a Spanish-speaking community prompted him, later in that year, to join a party of Americans who were setting out for New Mexico on the Santa Fe Trail.[1]

Alvarez established a business in Santa Fe, applied for Mexican citizenship, and over the next several years made repeated buying trips to Missouri. No likeness of the man seems to have survived, but documents of this period describe him as being small, five feet two inches tall, beardless, and of fair complexion.[2] *In 1829 he was among more than a dozen native-born Spaniards residing in New Mexico who were expelled from the Mexican Republic, a feeble measure taken in retaliation against Spain because the former mother country refused to recognize Mexico's independence, won in 1821.*

Manuel Alvarez spent his exile trapping furs with mountain men in the central and northern Rockies. He attended the summer rendezvous on the Green River in 1833, but shortly after that he was back in Santa Fe, operating a store. His order of expulsion had

---

[1] Two useful biographical articles on Alvarez are Harold H. Dunham, "Manuel Alvarez," in *The Mountain Men and the Fur Trade of the Far West*, ed. LeRoy R. Hafen, 10 vols. (Glendale, Calif.: Arthur H. Clark Co., 1965-72), 1:181-97; and Thomas E. Chavez, "Don Manuel Alvarez (de las Abelgas): Multi-Talented Merchant of New Mexico," *Journal of the West* 17 (June, 1979): 22-31.

[2] Ralph Emerson Twitchell, *The Spanish Archives of New Mexico*, 2 vols. (Cedar Rapids, Iowa: Torch Press, 1914), 1:342.

evidently been rescinded. No sooner had he reopened for business than he resumed his yearly trips over the Santa Fe Trail.

In 1839 the United States government appointed Alvarez as its consul in Santa Fe, to represent and protect the interests of American businessmen. Mexico, however, declined to grant him an exequatur—that is, official recognition—apparently because the government was unwilling to have consular functions performed by men who were engaged privately in trade, as Alvarez was. Nevertheless, the Mexican authorities allowed him to serve as acting consul and to carry out the normal duties of that office.[3]

Late in October of 1841 Alvarez experienced difficulties as he prepared to leave Santa Fe for the United States. The previous months had been turbulent ones in New Mexico, largely as a result of the expedition that had arrived from the Republic of Texas. The leaders claimed that they were on a peaceful mission to open commerce with the New Mexicans, but Governor Manuel Armijo chose to regard them as invaders, bent on conquest. He captured the entire Texas–Santa Fe Expedition and sent its members to Mexico as prisoners.

The incident aroused the local populace against American merchants, who were thought to be sympathetic to the Texans. At least two Americans were murdered, others had their possessions plundered, and Alvarez himself narrowly escaped assassination.[4] *In this hostile atmosphere, Governor Armijo refused to issue Alvarez a passport, a necessary document to permit him to leave for the United States. The delay nearly cost the consul his life.*

By the time he finally obtained the requisite papers, the season was far advanced. Winter crossings of the trail, with their everpresent threat of blizzards, were much to be feared, and Alvarez would not have made the attempt had another choice been open to him. All went well until the party reached the crossing of Cotton-

[3] Ralph G. Lounsbury, "Materials in the National Archives for the History of New Mexico before 1848," *New Mexico Historical Review* 21 (July, 1946): 250–51. Many years ago a copy of Alvarez's commission as consul came into the hands of Charles F. Lummis, who printed it in his *Mesa, Cañon and Pueblo* (New York: Century Co., 1925), p. 462.

[4] Details of these and similar happenings, as revealed in the consular dispatches of Alvarez, can be found in Harold H. Dunham, "Sidelights on Santa Fe Traders, 1839–1846," in *The Westerners Brand Book, 1950,* ed. Harold H. Dunham (Denver, Colo.: University of Denver Press, 1951), pp. 265–82.

wood Creek, located in present Marion County, Kansas, a well-known trail site about midway between Turkey Creek and Lost Spring. There a fierce snowstorm struck, which lasted for two days. Details of the disaster that ensued are contained in Alvarez's report to Secretary of State Daniel Webster, which was written on February 2, 1842, after the consul had arrived in Washington. Alvarez had continued on to the capitol to give the secretary timely information about recent developments in New Mexico. He may also have traveled to Philadelphia and New York to make purchases for his Santa Fe store.

The misfortune of the Alvarez party at the Cottonwood became part of the lore of the trail. Josiah Gregg, in his classic Commerce of the Prairies, *speaks of it in terms of outrage, placing blame on Governor Armijo, who, out of pure spite, held up Alvarez's passport.[5] In 1852, James L. Collins, summarizing the most notable episodes involving a freeze out on the Santa Fe Trail, devoted special attention to the Alvarez case.[6] Copies of Alvarez's report, here published in full for the first time, are preserved in the National Archives.[7]*

Having long since intimated to the Government of New Mexico my contemplated journey to the United States, and lately requested a passport (Sept. 29th), it was denied me, though I had used every means in my power to obtain it, having even interested persons in my favor who had influence, and were on good terms with his excellency the Governor [Manuel Armijo].

I could account for the motives of his refusal only by supposing he wished to procrastinate our departure until the season would be so

[5] Josiah Gregg, *Commerce of the Prairies,* ed. Max L. Moorhead (Norman: University of Oklahoma Press, 1954), p. 163.

[6] Collins's summary is published below, as document 2.

[7] Dunham, in "Sidelights on Santa Fe Traders," cited above, prints the introductory and concluding paragraphs of Alvarez's brief account of the storm at the Cottonwood, but he omits the main body of the report. The complete text is located in two collections of the National Archives, Washington, D.C., the first in Consular Dispatches, Santa Fe, New Mexico, General Records of the Department of State, Record Group 59, Aug. 28, 1830–Sept. 4, 1846; and the second, also in the General Records of the Department of State, Claims against Mexico, Commission of 1839, Claim 66, of Manuel Alvarez et al. of Santa Fe. In both cases the report is incorporated in a cover letter, Alvarez to Webster, Feb. 2, 1842.

far advanced that we must perish in crossing the plains, and if we followed the timbered creek rivers, it would prove extremely dangerous for so small a party (15 or 16 in number), it being almost certain that we should encounter large encampments of hostile Indians.

Being strongly solicited by the resident Americans of New Mexico to represent their wrongs in person to our Government and yielding to my own inclinations, I made a last effort to succeed, or bring matters at once to a close. I made some arrangements, bought mules, and provisions for the destitute men [of my party] who I thought would be liable to the most cruel persecution [by the governor, if they remained in New Mexico] (if for no other reason than that of wounding the feelings of the American merchants of Santa Fe) and started without leave, a company of 15 Americans, on the 25th October.

So soon as my people had started, I went to bid adieu to Mr. [Guadalupe] Miranda, the Secretary of the Government of New Mexico. His Excellency, the Governor having been informed of my visit, and my purpose sent for me by Mr. Miranda and after a short conversation directed that a passport should immediately be given to me. I left Santa Fe on the 26th October, the weather cold and stormy.

We made our way suffering from the inclemency of the weather, without other accidents than those of losing animals, until we arrived at little Arkansas: the Pawnee Indians that we met [there] letting us pass without much difficulty.[8]

On the 22nd November five of our members left and started down the Arkansas to Fort Gibson.[9] Four others left us hoping to reach the settlements in Missouri, a few days sooner than I could.

On the 24th reached the Cotton-woods Fork and found two of the four men who had started in advance for Missouri; the other two having continued. Same night had a severe snow storm, which continued for 48 hours with such violence we were unable to keep a fire. Snow 3 feet deep, we were all more or less frozen.

27th one of the two men [Seneca South, since dead] who had started in advance, returned to the camp badly frozen, and reported

---

[8] The Little Arkansas crossing, southeast of present Lyons, Kansas, was 234 miles from Independence, Missouri, according to Gregg's table.

[9] Fort Gibson, located in present-day eastern Oklahoma, was established in 1824 on the left bank of the Neosho (Grand) River, three miles above its junction with the Arkansas.

that his comrade, John Richmirs [?], had frozen to death four miles from the place of our encampment. Mr. South being so badly frozen as to be unable to travel, and one other of our men being sick, I concluded to leave them in camp with a man to take care of them, until we could send them aid from the settlements. The storm was so severe that many of my animals perished.

I arrived in Independence on the 13th December with 7 Americans and out of the 67 animals with which I started, I lost all except 27. On the 15th I started aid to the men left on the plains. On the 24th two of the men left [behind] arrived, the other had died a few days after I left them in Camp on the Cottonwood Fork. These sufferings and losses have all been the consequence of my detention after I had demanded my passport.

2. Report on Winter Travel, 1852

In 1852 President Millard Fillmore appointed William Carr Lane of St. Louis to be territorial governor of New Mexico. Lane was to replace the first governor, James S. Calhoun, who had died on the Santa Fe Trail a short time before, while returning to Kansas City. Lane, a noted physician and former army surgeon, had entered politics in 1823 and had won election as the first mayor of St. Louis, which had incorporated as a city in the previous year. He is said to have accepted office in distant New Mexico as a means of escaping some of the grief over the death of his sixteen-year-old son.[1]

At the end of July, 1852, Governor Lane left St. Louis by steamer for Independence, Missouri. There he transferred to a six-mule stagecoach for the beginning of his long journey to Santa Fe. At Fort Atkinson, west of Dodge City, he left the coach when he found that an escort of soldiers from Fort Union, under Maj. James H. Carleton, was waiting for him. These troops accompanied Lane to the capital of New Mexico, which he reached on September 9, forty days after leaving St. Louis.[2] Four days later he was sworn in as the second territorial governor.

On December 7, Lane delivered his executive message to the Territorial Assembly. In his message he discussed the problems and prospects of the region. Perhaps because he had just come over the Santa Fe Trail and therefore possessed firsthand knowledge regard-

---

[1] Stella M. Drumm, ed., "Letters of William Carr Lane, 1819–1831," Missouri Historical Society Publications (St. Louis), issued under the title *Glimpses of the Past* 7 (July–Sept., 1940): 52.

[2] Lane's diary of his experiences on the Santa Fe Trail is published in Ralph E. Twitchell, *Historical Sketch of Governor William Carr Lane* (Santa Fe: Historical Society of New Mexico, 1917). For Lane's additional references to the trail see Ralph P. Bieber, ed., "Letters of William Carr Lane, 1852–1854," *New Mexico Historical Review* 3 (Apr., 1928): 179–203.

ing its lack of conveniences, he made several pointed recommendations.

First, he urged the federal government to appropriate funds for the building of "caravansaries, or station houses, upon the Road to Missouri, 40 or 45 miles apart, to be kept by two or more citizens, who shall be married, and who shall furnish all travellers with shelter, (for man or beast) and good water and fuel, gratis—and other necessities, if practicable, for pay." The governor intended that these "simple and inexpensive structures" should serve as places where those who were crossing the Santa Fe Trail could take refuge from Indians or from the "horrors of winter storms."

Second, he recommended that the government drill wells on those sections of the trail where water was scarce. He particularly had in mind the Cimarron Cut-off, whose first fifty-six miles in southwestern Kansas, between the Arkansas and Cimarron rivers, was virtually a desert, known as the Jornada. The governor ventured the opinion that "a quick-sand, abounding in water, may be reached [by drilling] at a depth under 80 feet."

Third, he proposed that the then-monthly stage and mail service between Missouri and New Mexico be expanded to bimonthly service and then, as soon as the station-houses had been built, to weekly. Unfortunately for travelers, federal authorities paid no heed to Governor Lane's suggestions for station houses or wells. However, better stage service, provided by private contractors, did appear within a short time.[3]

After Governor Lane had delivered his speech and was preparing it for publication, he asked James L. Collins, a Santa Fe resident and owner of the Gazette, to send him a report outlining problems associated with winter travel on the Santa Fe Trail. Collins, a Kentuckian born in 1800, first traveled the trail in 1827 in the company of a pack train. From New Mexico he continued on to Chihuahua, Mexico, the following year and opened a mercantile business there that prospered until the outbreak of the Mexican War in 1846. After serving in the United States Army, he settled in Santa Fe and in June, 1851, founded the Gazette, the first long-lived

---

[3] Lane's speech was quickly published as a fourteen-page pamphlet by the office of the *Santa Fe Gazette*. The only copy that has thus far been located is preserved in the Benjamin Read Collection, New Mexico State Records Center and Archives, Santa Fe. Read printed extracts from the speech in his *Illustrated History of New Mexico* (Santa Fe: New Mexico Printing Co., 1912), pp. 488–93.

newspaper in New Mexico. He later served as Indian agent for the territory. He was murdered during the robbery of his Santa Fe office in 1869.[4]

Collins, owing to his extensive experience in freighting goods from Missouri, was thoroughly familiar with the stories that commonly circulated among merchants and teamsters about "the horrors of winter storms," as the governor had phrased it in his remarks to the Territorial Assembly. Therefore, he had little difficulty in preparing a report, in the form of a letter, that apprised Lane of some of the more celebrated cases in which caravans had been caught in blizzards. That document appeared as part of the appendix in the published version of the governor's message.[5] *As Collins noted in the last paragraph, his recital of winter hardships was designed to attract the attention of Congress, with the hope that it would pass an appropriation for the construction of the station houses along the Santa Fe Trail that Governor Lane recommended.*

Santa Fe, N.M.
December 10, 1852.

Dear Sir:

In answer to your inquiry on the subject of the practicability of a winter trip across the plains, from the frontier of Missouri to New Mexico, I have to say, that my acquaintance with the route in question commenced in the year 1827. Previous to that date, I believe but one attempt was made to cross the plains in the winter, and that was in the year 1824 or 1825, by a small party from St. Louis, at the head of which was Messrs. Faulkner and Anderson. They reached a point on the Arkansas River, near Chouteau's Island, when they were met by a heavy fall of snow, in which nearly all their horses and mules perished, and they were compelled to winter on an island that has since been known as "Log Island," from the quantity

[4] A short biographical sketch of Collins is provided by William A. Keleher in *Turmoil in New Mexico, 1846–1868* (Santa Fe, N.Mex.: Rydal Press, 1952), p. 484.

[5] Portions of Collins's report to Lane were incorporated by the Rev. J. B. Salpointe in his *Soldiers of the Cross* (Banning, Calif.: St. Boniface's Industrial School, 1898), pp. 107–9, but the full document has not been reprinted until now.

of timber cut for the subsistence of the few remaining animals, and to shelter the men from the storm.[6] After this, it was for a number of years deemed impracticable to attempt the trip in the winter, but since the route has become better known, it has been frequently travelled, often, however, resulting in great destruction of property, and not unfrequently of human life. In the month of December, 1841, Don Manuel Alvarez, an experienced and enterprising traveller, with a small party, was caught in a snow-storm, on Cotton-wood Creek, near Council Grove. In a few hours, two men and all his mules were frozen to death, and the snow drifted in such torrents as to extinguish the fires in a very few minutes. All hope seemed to be at once shut out from the party; everything of life around them had perished, and they themselves seemed fast sinking into an everlasting sleep. Two of the number, the stoutest among them, had sunk to rise no more, and the remainder would unquestionably have shared the same fate but for the energy of Mr. Alvarez himself, who, by absolutely driving the men into motion, was enabled to keep them alive until the storm had abated. Many of them, however, were badly frozen.

Few scenes have been presented to the view of men, more terrific than the one encountered by this little party on that dreadful night.[7] About the same period another party under the charge of Don Antonio Roubidoux [Robidoux], met a snow-storm at the same place. They lost in one night over 400 mules and horses, and one or two men, and narrowly escaped the loss of their entire party.[8]

In 1844, Dr. H. Connelly and Mr. Spyre, as early in the season as the 12th of October, encountered a storm near the Arkansas

[6] The account here, partially garbled, seems to refer to James Baird and Samuel Chambers's party from St. Louis, which was caught in a blizzard and remained for three months encamped on an island in the Arkansas River during the winter of 1822/23. The site was about five miles west of Dodge City, considerably downriver from Chouteau's Island. Among the partners in the expedition were William Anderson, Sr., Paul Anderson, Jr., and John Foughlin, who may have been the "Faulkner" referred to by Collins (see Louise Barry, *The Beginning of the West* [Topeka: Kansas State Historical Society, 1972], pp. 108–9).

[7] Details of the Alvarez episode are given in document 1 above.

[8] It is known that Antoine Robidoux of St. Louis made winter crossings of the Santa Fe Trail in 1824 and again in 1825. The disaster that Collins refers to probably occurred on one of those trips. For his biography, consult William S. Wallace, *Antoine Robidoux, 1794–1860* (Los Angeles, Calif.: Dawson's Bookshop, 1953).

River, in which a number of mules perished, and the remainder were only saved by running them into the timber on the river, a distance of some 15 miles.[9]

The same party, a few days subsequently, met a second storm, on the Cimarron, in which they lost in one night over 300 mules, and were compelled to remain until mules were sent from Santa Fe to their relief.[10]

In 1848, Messrs. Waldo, McCoy & Co., Government freighters, on their return trip to Missouri lost nearly all their cattle, amounting to 8 or 9 hundred head. The wagons were left on the plains until spring.[11]

In 1849, Messrs. Brown, Russell and Co., in crossing the Jornada from the Arkansas to the Cimarron, with a train of some twenty wagons, were overtaken by a storm of snow and sleet accompanied with a terrific wind.[12] The men retreated to their covered wagons, leaving the cattle to wander whither they would; but they instinctively kept within the inclosure formed by the wagons; they perished, however, in a few hours.

The snow drifted into the wagons through every crevice until they were filled nearly to the tops of the bows; this fortunately sheltered the men beneath from the piercing cold without. Two of the men ventured, about day light, to get out of their wagon for the purpose of kindling a fire, but in a few minutes became so stiffened with the intense cold, that they were unable to get into their wagon again without assistance. The others prudently kept beneath their

[9] Henry Connelly, who was, like Collins, a practicing physician, entered the Santa Fe trade in 1824. From 1828 to 1848, while residing in Chihuahua, he made numerous trips over the Santa Fe Trail. Later he served as governor of New Mexico during the Civil War. Albert Speyers (whose surname had various spellings) was a Prussian Jew who freighted goods between Missouri and Mexico. At the outbreak of the Mexican War in 1846, he briefly became a gunrunner, carrying arms and ammunition to New Mexico's Governor Manuel Armijo.

[10] The caravan suffered its loss of draft stock at or near Willow Bar in the Oklahoma Panhandle, a well-known site where the Santa Fe Trail crossed to the south bank of the Cimarron. The skulls and bones of the mules remained a landmark for many years; passing teamsters would arrange them in different patterns on the ground.

[11] The firm of Waldo, McCoy & Co. had its headquarters in Independence, Mo. David Waldo and William McCoy, who were prominent businessmen of that city, operated freight wagons and mail stages over the Santa Fe Trail. McCoy served as the first mayor of Independence from 1849 to 1850.

[12] In 1849 James Brown and William H. Russell formed a partnership for the purpose of transporting military supplies from Fort Leavenworth to New Mexico.

blankets and canopy of snow during the whole day and succeeding night, not venturing to change their position, wisely determining to endure the pangs of hunger rather than run the risk of sharing the same fate of their unfortunate animals.

On the second day the storm abated, though the cold was still intense. They ventured from their covers to look upon the sad wreck of life around them, and to think upon the awful condition in which they were placed—a condition which none can realize but those who have experienced it. Hundreds of miles from any civilized habitation, in the midst of a desert waste producing not a stick of timber in a range of many miles, and no animal left, they seemed to be shut up by an inexorable destiny.

One consolation was left them, the train was loaded with provisions, and they could use the wagons for fuel. But for this, they must all soon have perished; they were, however, enabled thus to sustain themselves until succor arrived in the spring.

In 1850, the same company with a large train of wagons with Government freight encountered a snow-storm between this place and San Miguel [N. Mex.], in which they lost over a thousand head of cattle. For this loss they have a claim now pending before the Congress of the United States.[13]

In the year 1851 the Cotton-wood Creek was again the scene of a terrible destruction of life. A Government train that had been started to the States by Col. Sumner, was overtaken by one of those destructive storms so frequently met with at that ill-fated spot; in a single night nearly three hundred mules perished; one man was also lost, and several others badly frozen.[14] In the same storm, the party in charge of the mail lost all their animals near Fort Atkinson, but were fortunately picked up by a train that had been more fortunate than themselves, and brought on to the Fort.[15]

[13] The caravan was caught in a mountain blizzard on the trail at the ruins of Pecos Pueblo, about twenty miles east of Santa Fe. James Brown rode to the capital to report to the garrison commander, but shortly after arriving, he died from a severe attack of typhoid fever and erysipelas (see Raymond W. Settle and Mary Lund Settle, "The Early Careers of William Bradford Waddell and William Hepburn Russell: Frontier Capitalists," *Kansas Historical Quarterly* 26 [Winter 1960]: 368).

[14] Lt. Col. Edwin Vose Sumner of the First Dragoons marched over the Santa Fe Trail in 1851 to assume command of the Ninth Military Department, which was headquartered in New Mexico.

[15] On Fort Atkinson see note 11 of document 6, below.

Other losses of life and property could be recited if it were deemed necessary, and to this I could also add a detail of the destruction of the lives and property of our fellow-citizens by the marauding savage tribes that have infested the route for the last thirty years, that would astonish the minds of the public, that the attention of the Government had not long since been directed to the subject.

Trusting that the representations of your Excellency may arrest the immediate attention of Congress, to the end that further and more ample protection may be given to this route, not only against the depredations of the Indians, but against the inclemency of the seasons,

I remain

With high consideration,

Your ob't serv't,

J. L. Collins.

His Excellency Wm. Carr Lane,
Gov. of Ter. of N.M.

3. Trail Letter
by Michael Steck, 1852

Dr. Michael Steck, the newly appointed agent for the Mescalero Apaches, left Independence on October 10, 1852, to assume his post in New Mexico. His ride over the Santa Fe Trail, which he described as "a rather eventful trip," took forty days. That was somewhat longer than a small party like his, composed of three carriages and three baggage wagons, usually required. The inclemency of the weather, occasioned by the lateness of the season, however, slowed the rate of travel.

Upon arriving in Santa Fe during the second week of December, Dr. Steck addressed a lengthy letter to an old friend, later a business associate, C. S. Biddle, who resided in Steck's hometown, Hughesville, Pennsylvania. In that document, Steck outlined in lively fashion his experiences in crossing the plains to New Mexico. Unhappily, only the first twelve pages of the letter have survived: the story breaks off just after the Steck party successfully weathers a blizzard along the Aubry Cut-off in southwestern Kansas.

Not only is the letter incomplete, it has suffered damage, which has caused holes on several pages. Notwithstanding these serious defects, what remains provides a valuable glimpse of trail travel in the early 1850s. Steck's description of the cooking of the head of a buffalo calf, a favorite dish of the mountain men, and his account of how plainsmen protected their livestock during blizzards serve to illuminate life in the western wilds. Words that are now missing in the original letter are indicated by underlined space in the published transcription. In almost every instance, the gaps are so small that the reader can guess the lost words or, at the very least, extract the meaning intended from the fragmentary sentence.

18

Dr. Michael Steck (courtesy University of New Mexico)

Michael Steck was born in Hughesville on October 6, 1818. He came from a long line of Lutheran ministers, but after considering a career in the church, he decided on medicine instead. In 1844 he graduated from Jefferson Medical College at Philadelphia, and during the next several years he practiced at the little town of Mifflinville, Pennsylvania. Apparently, his wife's failing health led him to accept his appointment by President Millard Fillmore to be the Apache agent for New Mexico, Steck's hope being that the salubrious climate of the Southwest might bring about a cure. In his letter to Biddle, at least in the part that is left to us, the author makes no mention of his wife, although presumably she was one of the three unnamed women he cites as being members of his overland party.

After ably serving the Mescaleros as agent, Steck was promoted to superintendent of Indian affairs for the New Mexico Territory.

Subsequently, he came into sharp conflict with Gen. Henry Carleton over treatment of the Indians, particularly the Navajos who were incarcerated at the Bosque Redondo Reservation on the Pecos River. As a result, he resigned the superintendency in 1865 and turned his attention to gold-mining investments in partnership with Stephen B. Elkins, who later became a United States senator from West Virginia.

With a small fortune made in New Mexico mining, Steck returned to his native Hughesville and built a mansion. [1] *He invested much of his wealth in local railroads; he also endorsed promissory notes for promoters and investors, a practice that ultimately left him bankrupt. After losing the mansion, he moved to a small farm near Winchester, Virginia, where he died on his birthday in 1883.* [2]

Santa Fe, N. Mexico
December 11, 1852

C.S. Biddle

Dear Sir:

I have at last arrived at headquarters after a journey of forty days from Independence. We have had rather an eventful trip and thinking that a few of the particulars might interest you I have concluded to give you a short sketch _____ allows me. A particular _____just received a communication from the Governor requesting me to be in readiness to take a trip to the North and Eastern part of the territory to visit our Red Brethern and hold talks with the tribes that live in that part of the territory. The Utahs, the Apaches and Hickarillas [Jicarillas].

Our party consisted of 18 men, 3 women and two children. We bought our outfit near Independence. Three six mule teams for Baggage and provisions and three carriages and several animals to ride upon. We started on the 10th October. Traveled ten miles. Next

---

[1] The biographical details presented here are drawn largely from a sketch of Steck's life provided by Keleher, *Turmoil in New Mexico*, pp. 506–7.

[2] The letter is preserved in the Michael Steck Collection, archive 134, box 1, Special Collections, Coronado Room, Zimmerman Library, University of New Mexico, Albuquerque. Dr. Steck's papers were presented to the university by his descendants in Winchester, Virginia, through the intercession of New Mexico's late Senator Clinton P. Anderson.

day we laid still in order to procure some things that we had forgotten. The 11th was a fine day and we amused ourselves shooting grouse (prairie chickens) which I can assure you are fine eating particularly when you superintend the cooking of them yourself. Next morning we started again in fine spirits but before noon it commenced raining and for the next six days it rained every day and I can assure you a heavy rain in October is far from being pleasant particularly on the prairies.

Seventh day we arrived at Council Grove. Here we rested two days; amused ourselves looking at the Caw [Kaw] Indians who were assembled for the purpose of receiving their annuity. Witnessed a number of their singular customs among which was their Buffalo Dance and scalp dance. On our arrival _____ a party returned from _____ against their enemies the Shawnee. Brought in one scalp which created great excitement and general rejoicing. After being very hospitably entertained for two days by the Methodist missionary stationed here, we proceeded on our journey and in the afternoon of the first day we were caught in a most tremendous rain storm. A man who has not experienced a storm on the prairies can form no idea of their severity. On this occasion our mules refused to face the storm, turned their tails to the wind and stopped short. We were compelled to encamp on the prairie without wood. Made our suppers upon Hard Bread and some cold meat we happened to have cooked. The wind fell about sundown when we pitched our tent, made our beds and slept soundly until daylight raised camp and traveled twenty miles to Cottonwood Creek. The storm still continuing and the road being heavy, we were unable to reach camp before eight o'clock at night. Imagine our difficulty. The night was cloudy and no moon. We finally, however, succeeded in fixing upon a camping place though in great danger every minute of upsetting our waggons into some gully of which the rolling prairies are washed full by the heavy rains. Now came an interesting scene. The raining had ceased and we had reached wood & water. Everyone went about his work with the most perfect good cheer, whistling and singing as though nothing uncommon _____ though we had lived since the night _____ upon crackers. In half an hour however our animals were picketted out in the best grass, a fine camp fire kindled, Camp Kettles, Skillet, frying pan, and coffeepot were brought into requisition and before eleven o'clock we were seated around our fire eating

our suppers with a relish that people who live in houses know
nothing about. Next day it was thought best to rest our mules and we
amused ourselves shooting ducks and geese which we found in great
abundance. Also four Turkeys of which we killed two very fine
ones. Our cook was busy all day cooking for the road as we knew we
were to see no more wood for the next two days. Next morning we
left camp at daylight and traveled 25 miles to Big Turkey Creek
where we had the good fortune to find fine grass for our stock. The
weather was fine and we were congratulating ourselves upon the
prospect of an undisturbed night's sleep until near sundown when a
moving object was observed upon an eminence some two miles off
and upon examination through a telescope it was found to be an
Indian we supposed reconnoitering our camp. We were still in the
country of the Osages and supposed he was examining into the
probability of his being able to creep upon us at night to steal mules.
We _____ doubling our Guard and urging the necessity of _____
watch. We recapped our rifles and spread down our Blankets &
Buffalo Skin _____ and slept soundly until four o'clock in the
morning when all hands were called and before six we were again on
the road towards the little Arkansaw which was twenty-five miles
distant. The morning was cloudy and threatening and we had not
traveled over ten miles when it commenced snowing. The wind blew
as it always does in a storm on the prairies, a perfect Hurricane, and
on this occasion from the N. East. We urged our animals to their
utmost speed in the hope of reaching shelter before the road would
become obscured. We were upon a high prairie without a landmark
to guide us and the snow fast filling up the road. It was already 4
inches deep and still falling thick and fast. We were about to despair
of reaching the river when to our great delight the clouds broke away
and the storm ceased and by two o'clock we safely encamped on the
bank of L. Arkansaw.

Excepting that it was very cold, we spent a pleasant night at the
Little Arkansaw & for the next two days we had fine weather and
nothing worth noticing occurred except that on the first day we killed
a Buffalo. The third night we reached Walnut Creek. For the last two
days we had seen numerous herds of Buffalo. In the afternoon I went
on in advance of the party to select a camp and kill another Beef as
near camp as possible in order to save time. Fortunately found a
large herd feeding immediately upon the Bank of the Stream. After

considerable trouble to get to the windward I crawled upon them and selected from perhaps 5000 Cows & Calfs the finest yearling and dropped him, reloaded my rifle without raising and spotted a two year old and brought him also. I had now all the meat I wanted and immediately proceeded to select a camp. Here for the first time in six days we had wood enough to make a good campfire. It was very cold and during the night we had a fall of snow two inches deep. But notwithstanding the unpleasantness of the weather our party seemed determined to enjoy what we seldom do on the plains, a good fire. Midnight found many of them seated around it telling stories and wasting choice pieces of the calves I had just killed.

The Cook was also preparing one of their heads for our Breakfast. A Buffalo Calfs-head is considered a great luxury by the mountaineers. The following is the mode of cooking them. We dig a hole in the ground large enough to bury whatever is to be cooked, build our fire in and over it to heat the Ground & if the piece of meat is large such as a turkey, Goose or Calfs-head we heat stones red hot and put them in the bottom, place the meat upon them and cover it over six inches deep with hot ashes then build the camp fire upon it and let it remain till morning when it will be finely cooked. Then with a stick you roll it out and remove the skin when it is ready to commence upon. I wish you could have been with us that morning seated upon the ground around our Calfs-head. I know you would have been delighted with your breakfast and ready to join me in denouncing a roast, _____, a stew or fricassee so long as you could have a Calfs-head cooked as I have just described.

We finished our breakfast and again were on the road. Traveled twenty miles and encamped on Ash Creek near the great Bend of the Arkansaw. Here we were visited by 40 or 50 Osages who were hunting Buffalo. We were greatly annoyed by them. They were very impudent and them being in such number made us apprehend danger at least of their stealing our animals. About sundown our fears were greatly increased by the appearance of moving objects immediately upon the Santa Fe road. At first we supposed them to be Indians but upon looking with the Glass we found they were waggons which was a great relief. In an hour more a paymaster in the army and an escort of dragoons drove up and encamped with us. Our number was then doubled. With this additional force, our fears were removed. We were then quite brave and immediately ordered them [the Indians] to leave our camp. They left and we immediately set to work fixing for a storm, some to getting wood to keep up a fire, others to picketing the mules in the best shelter in the ravines or to the leward of the bushes along the creek to shelter them from the storm. Tied down the waggon sheets, put extra pins in the tent and fastened doubly by securing it with a guy rope. The storm came but not so severe as we expected. The snow fell 3 inches deep but before morning it cleared off from the north.

Next morning, although it was excessively cold, we started before sunrise. Made a drive of 22 miles and encamped. We continued on for four days without anything to interrupt us except an occasional squall of snow. We killed several Buffalo and occasionally a Wolf when we thought he showed too much impudence. They are generally shy but we see immense numbers of them. A common thing to see [is] 50 at a sight and in the region of the Buffalo. In the daytime never out of sight of them, see Hundreds in a day. They live upon the Buffalo, the calfs and old ones. They select _____ it down, surround it and keep snapping them in the hind leg until they hamstring them. This accomplished they get him down and frequently in an hour devour the largest Buffalo. On the evening of the fourth day from Ash Creek we reached Fort Atkinson.[3] Here we remained two days during which time we were very kindly treated by the officers in command. This fort is near the crossing of the Arkansaw. As [it] is the only point at which supplies can be had, we bought here as much corn as we could haul and paid 4.30 pr. Bu. Its exposed situation and difficulty of access necessarily make the prices of all supplies proportionately high.

We left Fort Atkinson and traveled three days following the Arkansaw river in the Valley through which no river runs. There was no snow, but the elevated prairies were covered. This drove the Buffalo into the Valley. To say we saw thousands would give an imperfect idea of their numbers and to say we saw One Hundred Thousand acres of land covered with them will give a better idea, but still would fall short of the truth. We had them on our route from the Little Arkansaw to the upper crossing of the _____ Rivers, near four hundred miles. Of course, we had plenty of meat.

We had some difficulty in crossing our waggons. The river from its head to its mouth is a bed of quicksand, and it frequently

---

[3] For information on Fort Atkinson, situated on the Arkansas River west of Dodge City, see note 11 of document 6, below.

happens that waggons go down in it. This happened to one of ours near a hundred yards from the shore. The water was near waist deep but we had no alternative but to unload our waggon and carry everything ashore. This accomplished we succeeded with some difficulty in getting out our waggon. We encamped upon the bank of the stream and next morning made an early start upon a new route from the Arkansaw to the Cimarron, never traveled before last summer.[4] We had a plain trail to follow and had been told that from the river to Bearcreek, the nearest water, was 22 miles. We traveled leisurely as we expected to camp as soon as we reached the creek, but late in the afternoon when we reached it to our surprise and consternation we found it perfectly dry. We therefore made no stop. We were here told that eight miles farther on we could get water by digging. We arrived at the place after sundown, dug for water but as before the creek was dry. It was now dark and we were compelled to encamp without water. We succeeded in getting into a hollow that sheltered us from the northeast wind which was blowing fiercely. We picketted out our animals near camp and were busy talking about the prospect for a supper. Not a drop of water in camp nor had we any on the road for _____. Our real situation together with the uncertainty of reaching water on the following day together [with] the almost certain prosopect of a snow storm made our situation anything but pleasant. While we were thus engaged talking about our situation one of our pueblo Indian friends observed that about two miles back on the Creek while looking for water, he saw some snow in a ravine. We immediately dispatched two men and in an hour they returned with each a sack of snow upon their mules. Our greatest want was now supplied. With a few dry willows & weeds, we soon melted snow enough to make a cup of coffee for each one. We made a comfortable supper upon Hard bread and coffee not having fire enough to cook meat. The balance of the snow was melted and distributed among the animals, a quart to each. At ten o'clock all was quiet. Each one had wrapped himself in his blanket save the sentinels. At eleven your humble servant was called on guard. The night was dark and cloudy, the N.E. wind was blowing fiercely and I had not been at my post half an hour when the snow commenced

---

[4] Here Steck has reference to the Aubry Cut-off, a connecting trail between the Mountain Branch and the Desert Routes in western Kansas that was discovered by Francis X. Aubry. For additional details see note 10 of document 12, below.

falling thick and fast. In a few minutes the prairie was covered with a white fleece & our animals stood drawed up and shivering at the end of their picket ropes. At 12 o'clock I roused the camp to turn out and save our stock. To you who live in houses & sit chatting in a circle around a cheerful hearth and before retiring have your beds aired can hardly believe that a man under the circumstances I have just mentioned would get up at midnight and take the blankets that he himself was wrapped up in and place it upon his mule. But such was the fact upon this occasion. Our animals were brought up and placed to the windward of the waggons in a huddle and the men cheerfully deprived themselves of their _____ and blankets to save their lives. Safety depended upon our stock. If we lost it _____ left on foot in the middle of an immense prairie in a deep snow two hundred miles from the nearest habitation and at the time we knew not how far from wood and water.

After our mules were as comfortable as the circumstances would permit of, we all collected in one tent and, as no one thought of sleeping, one would tell how a government train of waggons was caught in a snow storm at the Cottonwood last winter and lost 200 mules and that the men in charge attempted to walk to Council Grove only forty miles, and two of them froze to death and others so badly frostbitten as to loose their limbs. Another how the mail party in December of last year lost all their animals in one night and the passengers were compelled to remain on the Cimarone six days without a particle of fire or cooked provisions until one of the men went to Fort Mackey [Mackay] and brought fresh stock.[5] Another how Spires in 1847 was caught on the Cimarone in a storm and was compelled to remain two months & lost every mule in his train, 175; that the men in order to save their lives burned up all his waggons.[6] Such were the topics together with suggestions and speculations with regard to ourselves if we lose our animals. But suddenly about two o'clock, a different turn was given to our thoughts for a moment. The accumulated weight of snow falling upon our tent together with the wind that was still blowing was too much for the guyrope. It gave way and suddenly down came the tent upon our heads. The first

[5] Fort Mackay, built in 1850, was a small post established on or near the future site of Fort Atkinson west of Dodge City.

[6] Steck's "Spires" was really Albert Speyers, whose winter misfortune on the trail was noted in document 2 above.

impulse was a roar of laughter. A second thought brought us to the conclusion that we were more comfortable where we were bearing the weight of the canvas together with a little snow than we would be in the storm. Therefore each one placed himself in as easy a position as he could get and made up his mind to remain there til morning. Directly some were asleep but not so with myself. I was listening to the storm and never was the cry of the sentinel, "Day is breaking," more welcome than upon that eventful morning.

4. James M. Fugate's Adventures, 1853

The call of the trail, with its promise of adventure, reached the ears of young James M. Fugate in the spring of 1853. He was then a resident of La Fayette County, Missouri, which lay on the western side of the state and was bounded on its northern edge by the Missouri River. Two decades before, the county's principal town, Lexington, had been a major outfitting point for Santa Fe caravans.

Although by 1853, places farther west, such as Independence and Westport, had assumed most of that role, still Lexington retained a small stake in the overland commerce with New Mexico. At least there was enough color and excitement when a wagon train formed up in front of the courthouse to entice youths from the town and the surrounding countryside, such as Jim Fugate, to sign on as a teamster.

Little is known of Fugate's career beyond what he recorded in his "Scouting Adventures in 1853." These adventures were either dictated or written down by the author late in life, after he had settled in Barton County, Kansas. That county, which lay astride the Great Bend of the Arkansas River and was cut by the Santa Fe Trail, already by the mid nineteenth century showed rich agricultural potential, a fact noted by more than one traveler on his way to New Mexico. Others besides Fugate would return in later years to carve out homes there.

In 1880 one Bernard Bryan Smyth, from the town of Great Bend, Kansas, who listed himself as a book and job printer, issued a small volume entitled The Heart of the New Kansas. *Besides business and governmental directories, he included therein assorted reminiscences of old-timers—among them, Fugate's "Scouting Ad-*

*ventures.'' Smith does not say whether he obtained the account
through an interview or from a written manuscript.*

*In recalling his experiences on the Santa Fe Trail almost thirty
years before, James Fugate remembered most vividly the series of
bloody fights with Indians that occurred as his caravan crossed
western Kansas. Some oxen trains managed by luck to get through
with scarcely a whisper of trouble, while others, his among them,
were practically under constant siege. Fugate's description of
finding a party of "Spaniards" from Santa Fe, who had been
massacred by Apaches and Arapahoes, and the subsequent battle
with the same Indians offers a sharp picture of the fierceness of
frontier conflict. All in all, his words are straightforward and
unvarnished. He makes no claim to personal heroics; rather, he
characterizes himself as an average young teamster who did his duty,
faced dangers of the trail unflinchingly, as was expected of every
man, and got his cargo through, to the delivery point in Santa Fe.[1]*

In April 1853, young, vigorous, and never having seen as much of
the world as generally fills the ambition of fellows in their early days
of manhood, I engaged as teamster to drive through with a train of
ox-wagons loaded with merchandise for the Santa Fe trade. We left
LaFayette county, Missouri, the 24th day of April; our company
comprised 45 men, armed with the old-fashioned long-range rifles,
each a Colt's navy revolver and bowie knife. Our teams numbered
210 head of cattle, in all.

Kansas was then one vast wild plain, over which roving bands
of hostile Indians were constantly cutting off emigrant and freight
trains on their way to New Mexico and the Californias.

After leaving the settlement some distance, we overtook twelve
men with three wagons, who had discovered there was danger ahead
and were awaiting reinforcements before venturing farther. This
increased our fighting force to 57 robust, well-armed men.

[1] This document first appeared in Bernard Bryan Smyth, *The Heart of the New
Kansas* (Great Bend, Kans.: B. B. Smyth, Book and Job Printer, 1880), pp. 61–68.
The title page listed this book as volume 1, but a second volume was never published.
This document, as well as other sections of Smyth's book, was later reprinted in
Biographical History of Barton County, Kansas (Great Bend: Great Bend Tribune,
1912).

Our first serious trouble began after reaching the Arkansas Valley, at a point near where Hutchinson now stands, and where we had gone into camp about noon of May 21st.[2] While at dinner we were suddenly startled by the alarm cry, "Indians!"

Before we had got our teams and wagons fairly in corral, they were charging around us on their horses, yelling and firing like demons. Taken at such a dangerous disadvantage and surprise, we were just in that position which makes men fight with desperation, and instantaneously our rifles were pealing forth their notes of defiance and death to the dusky murderous foe.

We were completely encircled by the savages, who proved to be Comanches, swinging upon the opposite side of their ponies exposing but little of themselves to our aim by firing under their horses' necks. Their deadly missiles were soon playing havoc among our cattle. The poor creatures were madly surging and bellowing around, endangering us to a death beneath their feet, worse to be feared within the enclosure than the foe without. This new danger soon drove us outside the enclosure of wagons in full view of the Indians.

We had now fairly got our hands in, and were tumbling their ponies at a rapid rate. Few Indians after their ponies fell, escaped a rifle bullet. The Indians were narrowing their circle until twenty-five yards scarcely intervened between us. But the motion of their steeds unsteadied their aim until it was but random, while the closer they pressed us the more destructive became every shot we fired.

Such fighting could not last long. After the first few rounds the savages mostly substituted the gun with the bow and arrows. Finding themselves getting most terribly worsted in the combat, they made a dash to ride down and tomahawk us all in one death struggle. I tell you, then, we had no child's play. Outnumbered four or five to one in a hand-to-hand fight to the death is a serious thing. We were soon mingling together, but driven against the wagons, we could dodge or parry their blows with the tomahawk, while the rapid flashes from the celebrated "navy" in each man's hand, was not so easily avoided by the savage warriors. We made the ground too hot for them, and

[2] If Fugate and his party actually struck the Arkansas at Hutchinson, Kansas, then they had veered off the main Santa Fe Trail by some thirty miles. Ascending that river, they rejoined the trail in the vicinity of Walnut Creek, near Great Bend.

with yells of baffled rage, they broke and fled, carrying off all their killed and wounded but three, which they had to leave.

Now for the first time since the fight began we had time to take in our situation. One of the bravest and best of our comrades, young Gilbert, was shot through the heart while fighting the savages back with clubbed rifle, his revolver having missed fire. He lay as he fell, with his hand clenched around the stock of his gun as though he would take the weapon with his departed spirit to the other world where he might avenge his death upon the savages who had paid such a dear penalty for their last work. Many others of our company were wounded, two of them severely. The dead and dying ponies were scattered about on the prairie with the arms and accouterments of their savage owners about them; while several of our cattle were also dead and dying from wounds made by missiles aimed for us.

The remainder of the day was spent in burying our poor comrade on the spot made sacred by his life's blood (which we did as well as we could under the circumstances), caring for our wounded, and gathering up the spoils of the fight. We destroyed everything belonging to the Indians that we could not carry away, and along towards night-fall moved about a mile up the river, where we went into camp.

After the excitement consequent upon the fight began to subside, we had much to talk over about our chances of fighting our way with such a small force through the entire boundless plains before us to New Mexico. The future looked hopeless indeed, but J. W. Jones who commanded the outfit, swore he would go to Santa Fe, or go to _____.[3] We dare not show the white feather, then.

Fight on the Walnut

Our progress was necessarily slow. No adventure of any consequence happened until we reached the Walnut creek. Here we camped some 200 or 300 yards below the old trail, in a horse-shoe bend, on the west side of the creek. No event occurred during the night to show the presence of Indians; but about dawn of the next morning, as the guards were turning the cattle out of the corral to

[3] J. W. Jones has not been identified. But during the early 1850s, John S. Jones, in partnership with William H. Russell of Lexington, Missouri, was heavily involved in military freighting to Santa Fe.

graze, the Indians—Cheyennes, some 500 of them some mounted and more afoot,—immediately tried to get possession of the cattle. Those on foot engaged the guards, while those mounted tried to get between the cattle and the corral, thus cutting them off. The firing immediately roused the camp to arms; and in the face of the firing by the Indians we surrounded the cattle, and drove them back into the corral.

Then the fighting began in good earnest. At first we proved too much for them, and they retreated into a low sag south of the corral; but quickly returned with more desperate energy than at first. Then forming solid lines, six or eight deep, made a forced charge on the wagons from the south, yelling like demons, and firing through under the wagons. It never seemed as if so few men could withstand such an assault. Our men were prepared for them, however, and, firing from behind and under the wagons, gave them a warm reception as they came up.

At the east end they broke through and came into the corral; but of those who came through it is a question if any ever returned. They were immediately shot and clubbed with the guns. I broke my own gun-stock over the head of one of the miscreants. There were nine of them left within the corral dead. The Indians, seeing the fate that had befallen their comrades who went through under the wagons, began a hasty retreat, and were quickly followed by the entire pack as fast as they could run. They took refuge in a low range of sand hills along the Arkansas river, some 60 or 80 rods to the south, from which they emerged occasionally during the morning to harass us.

We followed them up toward the sand-hills, firing at them to the best possible advantage; but when we had got as far as the low sag, we were ordered to retreat to the wagons. Our wagon-master, after the dead Indians, outside and in, were all counted, reported 60 Indians killed. Our own loss was five killed and several wounded, none mortally.

There was another camp of 35 men, sent out by Majors & Russell of Missouri, about half a mile west; and about 9 or 10 o'clock they formed a line and came down toward the Indians.[4]

[4] William H. Russell was a party to various partnerships. In 1852 he formed a new one with William B. Waddell of Lexington, creating a mercantile and freighting firm. Alexander Majors joined them in 1854, launching the celebrated company of Russell, Majors & Waddell. Thus, Fugate would seem to have made a slip by referring to the Majors & Russell outfit in 1853.

Pawnee Rock (from The History of Jackson County, Missouri *[1881])*

Seeing this we formed line and advanced to join them, and move together upon the Indians. They, upon the other hand, seeing our movement, beat a hasty retreat across the river.

We buried our dead on a point between two draws a little southwest of camp; and about 2 o'clock broke camp, and in company with Majors & Russell's outfit, started westward.

About 5 or 6 miles west we had a slight brush with the Indians, but nothing serious until we arrived at Pawnee Rock, which we reached about 2 or 3 o'clock next day.

A wagon train circled on the Santa Fe Trail (after Josiah Gregg, Commerce on the Prairies, *ed. Max L. Moorhead [Norman: University of Oklahoma Press, 1954])*

Fight at the Rock

We camped about 200 yards to the south of the rock. Nothing unusual transpired during the night. About 8 o'clock next morning, just as we had brought our cattle up to the corral, and were yoking them up, a band of Cheyennes, to the number of about 300, suddenly made a dash from the north, part of the Indians coming in on each side of the rock, and immediately surrounded our corral of wagons, with a terrible war-whoop.

The usual manner of making such a corral was to form a circle with the wagons, running them as close behind each other as possible, with the left-hand or driver's side innermost. When the circle was complete, an opening the size of a wagon was left for a gate, which was closed by a single wagon just inside the circle, so placed that it could be run aside or back into the gap, or "gate." During the night, and times of danger, the cattle are kept within this enclosure or "corral," as it is called; at other times they were turned out to graze, in charge of several men. On the left-hand side of the wagon-bed, above the wheels, there was a small box about five feet long, prepared with a hinged cover that pitched so as to shed rain. This box contained, in a convenient position, the arms, ammunition, lunch, trinkets, etc., of the driver.

Leaving our cattle just as they were, some yoked, some partly yoked, we instantly seized our weapons and pitched in vigorously to repulse the assault.

The Indians opened a heavy fire from the start. They made strainers of our wagon-boxes by perforating them with bullets and arrow-heads. The Indians who were mounted fired high, and may possibly sometimes have hit some of their own men on the opposite side of the corral.

After firing in this way for a while, and finding they could gain nothing, they beat a hasty retreat to the south, taking with them their dead and wounded, who were in nearly all cases tied to their ponies, as was shown by the thongs that lay by some of the dead ponies, where the riders had cut loose and got away.

In this fight we had one man wounded, and several cattle killed.

From here on we had to fight the Indians every few days. We had engagements at Pawnee Fork, again near Dodge, again at Cimarron, here by the Apaches and Arrapahoes, again at Mount Aubrey, Kearney Co.[5]

Fight at Mount Aubrey

At this place we arrived the next day after the slaughter of a party of Spaniards who were going east from Santa Fe, to purchase goods. We found ten dead Spaniards, and one wounded still living, with his scalp off, though he died the morning after.

At the first peep of day, the next morning after we arrived there, the Indians—Apaches and Arrapahoes—attacked us, first firing on the guards, and then coming up by slow, cautious movements, seeking every buffalo-wallow, or other slight protection to cover

[5] Today, there is no feature known as Mount Aubrey in Kearny County, Kansas. It seems plausible to assume that Fugate meant the elevation five miles west of the modern town of Lakin that was originally known as Chouteau's Mound, which is now called Indian Mound. It was located on the north side of the Arkansas, opposite the famous trail landmark of Chouteau's Island. Not far upstream, the Aubry Cut-off forked to the southwest. For information on the man who blazed that route and gave it his name, see note 10 of document 12, below.

themselves. So stealthily and steadily did they advance that almost before we were aware of it we had eight men lying dead. All this time we kept up a vigorous and pointed fire, always aiming and firing with intent to kill.

About 10 o'clock, finding they could not capture our train, they retreated the way they came, leaving their dead on the ground. These, amounting to between 50 and 80, we piled up on the plain, and left for the coyotes and buzzards.

We remained here four days, and buried our dead and the Spaniards—19 in all—in one trench. In the meantime—and this we tell in a whisper—we amused ourselves at target-shooting, using for a target the head of some luckless Indian, which would be placed in all conceivable positions to be shot at.

We had some more fighting now and then until we reached Fort Bent, after which we were out of the hostile country; and reached Santa Fe in safety, with what we had left of men and animals. We lost no wagons, and carried our cargo entirely through.

5. Narrative by Hezekiah Brake, 1858

Young Hezekiah Brake, originally from England, was looking for economic opportunity when he left Minnesota in late 1857 and, with his wife, Lizzie, and their young daughter, traveled by steamboat down the Mississippi to St. Louis. In a strange city and without friends, he found life hard and work scarce. At last, in desperation, he accepted a job as a dairyman on a ranch in New Mexico. His employer, then in St. Louis, was not planning to depart for the Southwest until the following February. So until then, Hezekiah took a temporary position as a waiter in the hotel at the ferryboat landing in nearby St. Charles.

In his narrative, Brake variously identifies the New Mexico rancher who had hired him as Mr. Aleandro, Mr. A, or "Aley." This individual was the post sutler at Fort Union, where he spent most of his time; he also owned a ranch with dairy cows eight miles west of the fort. It was to run that establishment that he had engaged the youthful but reliable Hezekiah Brake. Other sources reveal that the individual in question was G. M. Alexander.[1]

The descriptive passages of Brake's account of his first crossing of the plains on the Santa Fe Trail possess a certain freshness and precision. Perhaps in part those qualities can be attributed to the author's English birth—the response of a well-educated foreigner to the exciting but grim realities to be encountered in the wilds of frontier America.

In the company of "Mr. A," Brake proceded to Council Grove, where his employer put together the outfit necessary for the trip to

[1] *Santa Fe Weekly Gazette*, July 10, 1858. Reference courtesy of Jacqueline Meketa, Corrales, New Mexico.

Hezekiah Brake at the age of thirty-three (from
Brake, On Two Continents)

Fort Union. Their preparations were aided by the prominent
merchant Seth Hayes, who was related both to the Boones and to Kit
Carson. On the night before their departure, the young man was
beset by gloom at the prospect of the dangers ahead and by thoughts
of his wife and child, whom he had left behind in Missouri.

The journey southwest, made in good time with fast mules, had
the usual allotment of adventures—meetings with parties of Kiowas
and Cheyennes, in which hostilities were fortunately avoided, and
the theft of Brake's boot by a wolf. Indeed, the author's brief
narrative is rich in those small episodes and details of prairie travel
that can create for the modern reader a vivid picture of life on the
open trail.

One month after leaving Independence, Brake reached Fort
Union. That arrival marked the end of his trail account, which
appears below. A short postscript, however, can be added.
Brake immediately rode west and took charge of the ranch and dairy
belonging to Mr. Alexander. He remained in that position for two
years, and during that interval, his wife and daughter came out from
St. Louis to join him. On the approach of the Civil War, the family
returned east, following the Mountain Branch of the Santa Fe Trail.
They got only as far as Council Grove, where Hezekiah decided to
stop, purchase land, and pursue farming. Soon he was selling the
produce of his gardens and fields to wagons passing along the road
to Santa Fe.

So far as I know, Hezekiah Brake spent the remainder of his
days in Council Grove. In later years he was regarded as one of the
pioneers of the community. No doubt at the prompting of others, he
set down his recollections of early New Mexico, which were
published as a book in 1896.[2] *From that, the following narrative is*
drawn. Toward the end of his recital he declared with eloquence
colored by nostalgia: "So long as a single person who once crossed
the plains over the Santa Fe Trail remains, so long will pictures of
that grand old time rise in his mind, and stand out in bold relief,
unchallenged as to wildness and beauty by any other scene of
imagination or memory."[3]

As the time drew near for my departure to New Mexico, I left St.
Charles, went down to St. Louis, and bade my loved ones good-bye.
The dangers of the journey were obvious enough to my own mind,
but I tried to leave as favorable an impression of it as possible with
my wife. The mother of Mr. Aleandro, or "Aley," as we called
him, was blind. To her the way seemed full of perils, and she
earnestly besought me to take care of her comfort and stay in her old
age—her beloved son. Although I was strong and hopeful, I was not
sure but my wife would have preferred the same request of Mr. Aley
concerning myself if she had seen him. In those days the women
dreaded, worse than death, the perils of the Western trails.

[2] Hezekiah Brake, *On Two Continents: A Long Life's Experience* (Topeka,
Kans.: Crane & Co., 1896).
[3] Ibid., p. 176.

We were to ascend the Missouri river to Independence, go from there to Westport, Missouri, and on across the plains to New Mexico. We accordingly took the train for Jefferson City, and caught a boat there in the night for Independence.

Imagine our feelings when the boat, within eighteen miles of our destination, stuck in the ice, and no amount of pressure could budge it an inch farther. Worse than that, the captain put up placards all over the boat as follows:

FIVE DOLLARS PER DAY
FOR ALL PASSENGERS STAYING ON THIS BOAT

There was nothing else to do but disembark. The "passengers" went ashore, secured a farm wagon as a conveyance, a farmer as a driver, and jolted into Independence about midnight. As for myself, I was so cold that I put my small baggage on my back, and walked most of the way. In the morning, we went on to Westport, where Mr. A. had a fine span of American mules. The next day we left for Council Grove, Kansas, the rendezvous of freighters and traders who were crossing the plains. Kansas City stands now near the old town of Westport, but, save for the Wyandotte Indians, there were few settlers then on this side of the river.

We started February 1, 1858, Mr. A. and myself driving his mules to a buggy.[4] We made half of the one hundred and forty miles the first day, sleeping at night with a settler named Barricklow. Only a shell of a house, the building was barely inclosed, and I suffered greatly from cold. After an almost sleepless night, I arose and went out to see after the mules. My teeth were already chattering with cold, and I did not speak to the animals as I passed behind them with a bucket of water. One of them kicked at me, missed me, but hit the bucket, and sent the icy water in a shower-bath all over me. As the freezing liquid splashed in my face, ran around my neck and down my spinal column, my initiation into the mysteries of freighting seemed complete.

Our fare settled, and the broken bucket paid for, we left this comfortable mansion. On the way to Council Grove, at the present

---

[4] Brake is careless in his reporting of dates, for he says here that he left on February 1, 1858, and at the end of his account he claims that he arrived at Fort Union on March 1, 1859. Since the journey clearly lasted for one month, not a year and one month, one of the dates is in error.

Burlingame, Mr. A. employed a man named Louis Boyse to accompany us across the plains. We reached Council Grove that night, and began our arrangements for the trip to New Mexico.

Seth Hayes, so well-known as the first trader in the present county of Morris, Kansas, kept a store and an outfitting station at Council Grove at this time. He had in keeping now six small Mexican mules, a good pony, a large wagon, and various other necessary acquisitions to our outfit. It took us four days to get the animals ready and lay in a supply of everything needful for our journey. An old negress who worked for Mr. Hayes roasted coffee, made cakes, and gave us a keg of pickles and sauerkraut as relishes.[5]

On the last night before we started, the prospect seemed especially gloomy to me. Far away from my wife and child, and six hundred miles of constant danger in an uninhabited region was not a pleasant prospect for contemplation. But I laughed with the rest, joked about roasting our bacon with buffalo chips, and the enjoyment we would derive from the company of skeletons that would strew our pathway.

The few business houses at this time were mostly log cabins, and there was very little attempt made by the citizens to follow the fashions; but there were dudes even then in Council Grove. One of these was not attired in a faultless broadcloth suit with buttonhole bouquet, eyeglass, and cane, but wore an elaborately trimmed buckskin suit fringed down the side. His attire was finished off with beaded moccasins—the artistic production of some Cheyenne squaw whose cunning hand had cut them "bias" at the toe and fringed them at the heel. He wore a broad-brimmed hat, and under it were heavy masses of unkempt hair. Upon either side of him hung a navy revolver, and a bowie-knife was stuck in his belt. He rode a richly-caparisoned mustang, and far surpassed the modern dude in appearance.

Amusement was not lacking, however, even at this early time. Besides the cowboys, there were the courts to furnish fun for the citizens, and even visitors or chance stayers in Council Grove had the stories of the time rehearsed for their amusement. I remember

[5] The black woman was Sarah (Aunt Sally) Taylor, who remained with Seth Hayes for many years after she was freed. Her grave is next to his in the Council Grove cemetery.

some of these stories caused much laughter as we sat listening to them around Mr. Hayes's fire.

A 'Squire Mansfield, then a squatter on the present site of Council Grove, tried a fellow for some misdemeanor, and he was found guilty. With much dignity the court sentenced the prisoner in the following announcement:

"The court stands adjourned. The constable now will march the prisoner to the nearest wet-goods establishment, and see to it that he sets up the liquor for attorneys, witnesses, and spectators. Boys, fall in!"

Another case as amusing was also related: B. F. Perkins, a talented young lawyer, was attorney for the plaintiff and a Colonel Sanford for the defendant. After the arguments were finished, His Honor delivered the following charge to the jury:

"Gentlemen, you have heard the evidence in the case. You have also listened to the words of the learned counsel for both plaintiff and defendant. If you believe what the counsel for the plaintiff has told you, then you'll side for him; and if you believe what the counsel for the defendant stated, decide for him. But, gentlemen of the jury, if you are like me, and don't believe what either of them said, then I'll be darned if I know what you can do. Constable, take charge of the jury!"

We went off in grand style the next morning. The huge prairie-schooner was well filled. We took with us for planting and feeding half a ton of shelled corn. Besides this, we had Hungarian-grass seed, rifles, boxes of crackers, bacon and sugar, robes, blankets, and many other articles—about two tons in all. Louis Boyse, a great fellow, bigger than the mule he rode, and myself, a small man, armed with a "blacksnake" whip, and riding a small pony, were the attendants. Mr. A. drove the six Mexican mules, and the American mules were tied behind the wagon. On the first day we only reached Diamond Springs, about twenty miles from Council Grove, and there camped.

We allotted thirty miles per day as our limit of travel, and usually made fifteen of them before breakfast. We would then camp, spend two hours cooking our breakfast and resting our horses, after which we would go fifteen miles further and stop for the night. At the close of the second day, we reached Cow creek, the last and only place of refreshment between Council Grove and Fort Union, New

Mexico. A man kept a whisky shanty here, and sold cheap liquor and dear oysters to travelers. Few passed his "house" without doing ample justice to both viands and spirits. At noon of our third day out, we wished the ranchero farewell, and as his dwelling disappeared in the distance behind us, we found ourselves upon the Santa Fé trail, away from civilization, our faces toward Fort Union.

That night we picketed our animals, fed them, secured everything, made a fire, cooked our bacon and coffee, and with the consoling reflection that we had no more wood, prepared for the night. Mr. A. slept in the wagon, and Louis Boyse and I rolled ourselves in blankets and lay down upon a buffalo-robe under the wagon and slept soundly until morning. We were hungry and dirty the next day when our fifteen miles were made, and as we had reached a small creek, we performed our ablutions, and admired ourselves as mirrored in the operation. Mr. A. complimented us upon our agility and cleanliness in preparing breakfast. Talk about the element named being next to godliness! The latter was a long way from freighters crossing the plains by the Santa Fé trail, if cleanliness was a condition of its nearness. The sand must have been as good as mustard, though, for we relished our late breakfast better than we ever had one eaten in a first-class hotel.

We made our usual afternoon drive of fifteen miles, turned out as on the previous night, cared for our stock, ate our suppers, and retired to our respective "apartments."

Two days later brought us to the Big Bend of the Arkansas river, where there were dangerous quicksands. We camped for the night, hoping that we would meet the mail outfit here and secure help in crossing. The wagon being heavily loaded, Mr. A. decided to relieve it by taking out half a dozen sacks of corn and hiding them. If we did not meet the mail until we were over the river, we would sell the corn to the mail-drivers at cost, as they were always glad of an opportunity to secure corn so far from civilization. The mail did not come, and we deposited the corn as directed in a low place near the river.

Mr. A. now mounted the pony, reconnoitered a little, and started to cross in a zigzag direction, in order to avoid the quicksands. We followed with the mules and wagon. The pony was hardly in the river until it nearly disappeared from sight. Of all the yelling, screeching and scolding I ever heard, those men did the best job! But their horrible din either conciliated the demon of the river, or else the mules understood their business, for one thing is certain— we crossed in safety.

"Don't you think you will need your lungs?" I asked, when we all stood panting on the other bank. "I have heard that down in New Mexico, lungs are considered essential to existence."

"Shut up!" growled Mr. A. "Mules always have to be frightened nearly to death or they will not cross the river."

I begged pardon in the London dialect.

I now rode my pony ahead of the team to the brow of the hill, and looked around me. Lo! Just beyond was the whole tribe of Kiowa Indians. Boyse turned pale, and I would have enjoyed the ice on Minnetonka better than my present situation. Mr. A. sung out, "See to your revolvers and knives! Don't be frightened."

We stopped the team and awaited the arrival of the Indians. It was a motley scene. There were chiefs, bucks, squaws, papooses, horses, ponies, robes, blankets, pots and kettles—all mixed up in a general "jamboree" of noise, commotion, odor, and color. They at once surrounded us. Being in a civil mood, they merely begged some powder and lead. We gave it to them, without first putting it in rifles, and attempted a further conquest of their savage hearts by opening boxes of sugar and crackers, and offering them a dainty repast.

In a few moments they moved southward, and we now toiled up the steep and sandy ascent, the poor mules panting and quivering from the exertion. I rode along on the pony, plying my whip in circles over their backs, and pitying the dumb brutes with all my heart. Looking back, I saw a squad of about thirty of the roughs of the tribe, both squaws and braves, with faces painted black, yellow and red, coming after us, I was sure for plunder. They immediately overtook us, and began to talk of robbing and killing us. We took no notice of them, and they accompanied us to the top of the sand-hills. Mr. A. could understand them, and he learned that they expected us to cook for them. They were told they could have some sugar and crackers. Accordingly, they disposed themselves in a circle on the ground. I got out a box of crackers, filled a washbowl with sugar, and waited upon the rascals. Delighted and satisfied with this rare feast of good things, they insisted on all of us lighting our pipes and smoking a pipe of peace together. The fumes of their "kinnikinic" did not deceive us. They meant mischief. Suddenly the biggest and ugliest of the bucks sprang up, and led the way to the supplies in our wagon. The rest followed him.

To be left without food and ammunition, or animals to carry us onward, two hundred miles from a human habitation, was far from pleasant. We resolved to sell our supplies dearly. As the first Indian set his foot upon our wagon-step, we made a simultaneous rush at them with drawn revolvers and flashing knives. Each of us dragged a rascal down, and I was about to stick my man when Mr. A. shook his head in a silent "No." The Indians were evidently unarmed, and the majority of them seemed to wait the action of their leaders. They saw we were going to defend our lives and our goods, and one of them sprang upon the tongue of the wagon, and laid his hand upon our rifles. Louis Boyse caught him and flung him upon his back. With an indescribable, guttural howl, the injured redskin crawled off, and closing around him, they all raised their war-whoop. Such a prolonged, relentless, blood-curdling yell as that unearthly, simultaneous shriek given by those thirty savage hoodlums, I had never heard. It was worse than the supposed cries of the condemned in the infernal regions. But with their accustomed respect for what they claim to possess in a marked degree—personal courage—they decided to yield us the victory, and retire from the field, which they did with much precipitation.

When the Indians were out of sight, I made a fire of buffalo chips, put the coffee on to boil, spread a blanket for a tablecloth on the lap of Mother Earth, and placed thereon some canned stuff in order to save time. (Blessings on the man or woman who first thought of canning eatables! The idea has kept many a traveler over the plains to Pike's Peak or Santa Fé from starvation.) We did not talk as much as usual around our hastily improvised table. Thoughts of home and loved ones, possible loss of life and property, suffering, or perhaps starvation on these arid plains if we escaped from the Indians, were some of the ideas that flitted through our minds.

As for myself, some way a garbled version of the affair was later carried to my wife, to Minnesota, and even to England. I was believed dead. Persons holding my property appropriated it to their own uses. My wife and child mourned for me as lost to them by death at the hands of the Indians. Yet while most of the friends who wept over my supposed decease are cold in death, I still live to write the story of that February day in 1859.

In about half an hour after the Indians left us, we were again on our way, moving as rapidly as possible. We had not gone two miles further until we met a band of Cheyenne warriors, in full war equipage. They were beautifully painted, and dressed in red. They carried long spears, bows and arrows, and paid no attention to us except to say "How!" A few miles further on, we met the mail. The men informed us that the Cheyennes were after the Kiowas, hence the rapid movements of both bands. We devoutly hoped that the artistically draped Cheyennes would overtake the picturesque Kiowas, and make them repent of having gorged our sugar and crackers! The mail-drivers assured us of their pleasure in getting the corn awaiting them, and that the rest of our way was free from danger. We were more cheerful after that news was imparted.

The little mules were now stiff from so much stopping, and Mr. A. ordered me to use the whip more freely. The Indians had mocked my driving performances that morning, and the memory of it, along with other insults they had offered, made the poor little mules suffer, I am afraid, for I took a sort of revenge by cracking my whip at them, in the absence of the burly braves whom I longed to punish in like manner. We made twenty miles further before dark, then turned out, picketed our animals, cooked our suppers over our smoky chip fire, and early retired to rest.

The air was becoming remarkably mild by this time. Travel, relieved from the fear of Indians, was delightful. We even thought of amusement. When we had traveled about ten miles the next day, I said:

"I wish we had some fresh meat."

"I have a good rifle," Said Mr. A., "and I am a sure shot. Do you like prairie dog?"

"It depends upon who cooks it," I answered.

"You shall cook it," replied Mr. A.

We were passing through a prairie-dog village. At the door of his habitation, a fierce young dog set up a yelp of remonstrance at our interrupting their councils, and Mr. A. silenced him with a bullet. Throwing the dog into the wagon, we went on to our limit of fifteen miles, and stopped for breakfast.

I had cooked 'possum, 'coon, even terrapin, in my time, and was not to be deterred by jeers from preparing fresh meat simply because there was no material at hand to cook but a prairie dog, and no fuel for a fire but buffalo chips. So I made my fire, put a vessel of water on to boil, and dressed the dog. A savory stew was soon prepared which threw fried bacon into the shade. All of us pronounced prairie dog superior to squirrel or rabbit, and declared that after this we would often have fresh meat.

We were near Pawnee Fork when we camped that night. After a good night's rest, undisturbed by dogged dreams or other reminders of our stew, we rose early, cleaned and greased our wagon-axles, and resumed our journey. We looked back at the sparkling water of the Ornado [Jornada] with regret. Before us lay a journey of fifty miles before we could hope to strike another plentiful supply of water.[6] I wondered, too, if the breezes that swept this high table-land could speak, what tales of snowstorms, of sand storms, of freezing and starving cattle, or perishing men, it would whisper in our ears.

We carried with us from our camping-place a supply of fresh water, and without breakfasting, made twenty miles. By this time we were again hungry for fresh meat. Mr. A. shot a fat young prairie dog as before, and I skinned the animal and prepared him for the pot. Being very lean myself, I have always been a great admirer of fat, and I testified to this admiration now by putting a piece of the stuff into my mouth. I had no more than masticated and swallowed that piece of fat until I was sicker than words can express. In disgust, I threw the whole dog away, and I have never since particularly cared for prairie-dog meat. As to the fat, that mouthful has lasted me through all of the years that have since elapsed. It took a strong cup of coffee to cure the dog fit from which we all seemed to be suffering, and bacon and eggs tasted like ambrosia. Louis laughed heartily, and insisted that I was attacked with hydrophobia; and Mr. A. said:

"You shall have an antelope in a day or two for your mess."

Never shall I forget the quantities of bleached bones upon the Ornado table-land! Tons of iron strewed the road, remnants of scenes when for temporary relief freezing men burned the wood-

---

[6] The party had taken the Cimarron Cut-off and was entering the desert between the Arkansas and Cimarron rivers in southwestern Kansas.

work of their wagons. Gloomy reflections would force themselves upon our minds when, almost without water, we camped for the night. But we were only ten miles from a fresh supply, and two or three hours' travel the next morning brought us to some beautiful springs. The earth was frozen around them, but the springs were open, and never had water seemed to us so delicious or precious.

Mr. A. declared we were now within the range of antelope, and as we approached the Cimarron river we caught several glimpses of these shy and beautiful animals. As we neared our camping-ground, he was fortunate enough to bring down a fine young kid. When we had camped for breakfast, we took a sack of buffalo chips—carried forward for fuel—made our fire, and for the first time in my life I had the satisfaction of cooking and helping to eat fried antelope-chops.

I had now ridden my pony three hundred miles: to say I was sick of riding, feebly expresses my feelings. I had been compelled to crack my whip at the poor little mules, too, until my shoulders were very lame. Some way or other, that was not all of my misery. The ghost of that antelope or some other mysterious influence affected me almost to tears. Suddenly I stopped the train. I could carry my vague regrets no farther. I must do penance for my sins. To my surprise, my companions were similarly affected. I said, languidly, "It is a good thing to be mutually agreed," and it was some minutes before my emotion or vomition would let me say more. When we had made our day's journey and stopped for the night, there were few words spoken. Nervous sympathy made words unnecessary. All we wanted was repose. We rolled up in our blankets in silence and fell asleep. Antelopes, graceful and fleet, flitted swiftly through my dreams; but I was as shy of them as they were of me.

For the first time during our journey, we stopped the next morning long enough to cook an early breakfast. I made some biscuits and some coffee. We partook sparingly, however; the lesson in intemperance had been too strongly impressed and expressed for us to fall again so soon.

We crossed the Cimarron that night, and drank a cup of tea on the opposite bank. Wrapped in our blankets, we lay down as usual to sleep, but something kept me awake: I did not know but what it might be prairie dog or antelope. Louis was the sleepiest-headed of mortals. Once asleep, nothing short of an earthquake would have disturbed him. As I slept lightly, and wakened easily, I always kept my boots and my only pony-bridle under my head, in order that I might be prepared for any emergency that might arise. I had just fallen asleep, when I felt something move under my head. I put up my hand: one of the boots and the bridle were gone. I sprang up in time to see in the dim light, the outline of a large wolf, but the yell I gave must have disconcerted his wolfship, for he ran, leaving the boot and the bridle. My companion knew nothing of it the next morning, and but for the condition of my property would have kept on insisting that it was all "a bootless dream." I had no fancy, however, to ride into Fort Union on a pony wearing a rope bridle, myself minus one boot, and I praised the fates that I had recovered my confiscated goods.

In two days from that time, without accident or incident, we had made sixty-five miles, and camped at the Rabbit Ear creek. A solitary Indian came up to us and warned us that there was trouble among the Utes, but we were more suspicious of him than of them, and watched him all night. We also met a second mail party here, and they reported the road clear. The climate was becoming very delightful, and when we had rested our mules, cleaned our wagon-axles, and bathed ourselves, we felt anxious to push forward to the next camping-ground, known to travelers by the trail name, "the Wagon Mound." It was about fifty miles to this point, and there was an abundance of water there, entirely free from alkali.

Often now small herds of antelope, evidently surprised at the invasion of their territory, lifted their pretty heads, and stared at us with their lovely dark eyes, scarcely moving from their tracks.

Mr. A., who was exceedingly fond of displaying his seventy-five-dollar rifle, at last called a halt, and looked knowingly at me.

"By all means," I said, answering the inquiry.

Mr. A. accordingly shot one of the beautiful creatures, and that day when we halted we turned our backs upon our past experience, and dined on antelope.

The road here was a fine example of what Nature could display in the matter of irregularities on the earth's surface. The noise and turmoil incident to getting the mules over this tract of rough country either digested our supper or else our theories of temperance better accorded with our practice, for this time we suffered no inconvenience, and slept soundly during the night.

Round Mound, a prominent landmark on the Cimarron Cut-off in northeastern New Mexico

The next stopping-place was known to freighters by the elegant name of "The Devil's Backbone," and for this classical retreat we started while the morning star was yet visible.[7] "Start the mules briskly," commanded Mr. A., "and keep them on the swing. If they are not kept warm they will cave in." So I plied my whip unmercifully. The big mules were very lame, and the little ones were in a pitiable condition. As for myself, I was no longer sick from riding—I was sore. Language cannot express my pity for the faithful dumb brutes, nor my own sufferings in my attempts to maintain a dignified position upon the pony. After three hours of rapid travel we camped, and made the wretched animals as comfortable as possible.

We were out of flour; so we soaked crackers and fried them, to eat with our slices of antelope, and then lay down and rested for two hours. Within ten miles of the "Devil's Backbone," a terrible wind- and sand-storm struck us. The sand not only filled our eyes, but all the air. We could not see each other or the mules. The latter were so frightened that we could hardly manage them, and they absolutely

[7] Brake's "Devil's Backbone" is not a familiar place-name on the Cimarron Cut-off. He seems to be referring to a basalt out-cropping between the Round Mound and Point of Rocks in northeastern New Mexico.

refused to advance. What would be the result should the storm continue any length of time, we could not foresee. It was impossible to cook, for we were without water; the darkness was most intense, and the terrific storm increased in violence each moment. We made the animals as safe as possible, and retired, cold and hungry, in a state of nervous depression impossible to describe.

But the storm did not last half the night. In the morning, all was safe, and the air was as fresh and balmy as in early spring-time. Our cheerfulness revived as we surveyed the heaped-up sand-drifts, and thought of the pleasure of plowing through them. But while we hitched up the mules I was thinking of the vicinity of the "Devil's Backbone," and asking myself if the proximity of Satan accounted for the sand being flung in our eyes and strewn in our pathway. The word "backbone" sent me off on another train of thought. We would emulate Job's patience, and travel on to a place of safety beyond the limits of his Satanic territory.

We traveled slowly now, for we were all nearly worn out, but we were certain if nothing happened, to reach Fort Union in three or four days. There were plenty of wateringplaces during these last stages of our journey. Point Rocks, Cold Springs and Wet Stone Basin were all passed, and with animals that had made better time than the mail—for we were only twenty-eight days on the road, including our delays on the Missouri river, at Independence, and Council Grove—we entered Fort Union March 1, 1859.[8]

---

[8] Regarding the date see note 4 above.

6. David Kellogg's Diary, 1858

The discovery of gold in Colorado in 1858 sent a flood of fortune hunters hurrying across the plains of Kansas to the foot of the Rockies. Since it was the shortest and most direct way to the gold fields, the Smoky Hill Route from Leavenworth through central Kansas bore the largest volume of traffic. But the Santa Fe Trail, even though longer, enjoyed popularity among some overlanders because it was well traveled and was amply supplied with water; also, its grass greened up two to three weeks earlier than that on the more northerly route. Kansas City, then the main departure point for the Santa Fe Trail, developed a fierce rivalry with Leavenworth in a bid to become the outfitter of parties bound for Colorado.[1]

Among those in the first wave of gold seekers was young David Kellogg, who kept a diary of his experiences on the trail.[2] *He is known to have left home at an early age and to have engaged in steamboating on the Mississippi River. In time he became an ardent abolitionist, and at least one source claims that he fought alongside John Brown in Kansas.*[3] *Near the beginning of his diary, Kellogg describes Brown's role in the Battle of Black Jack and casts interesting sidelights on that affair.*

In the entry for September 20, Kellogg notes his arrival at 110 Mile Creek (so named because it was 110 miles from Fort Osage,

[1] James F. Willard, "Sidelights on Pike's Peak Gold Rush, 1858–59," *Colorado Magazine* 12 (Jan., 1935): 3–13; and Calvin W. Gower, "The Pike's Peak Gold Rush and the Smoky Hill Route, 1859–1860," *Kansas Historical Quarterly* 25 (Summer 1959): 158–71.

[2] Kellogg's diary, in two parts, appeared in the publication of the Society of Sons of Colorado, *The Trail*, in December, 1912, and January, 1913. Copies were courteously supplied to me by the Colorado Historical Society, Denver.

[3] LeRoy R. Hafen, ed., *Colorado Gold Rush: Contemporary Letters and Reports, 1858–1859* (Glendale, Calif.: Arthur H. Clark Co., 1941), p. 79 n.

coward along the border, but his men stand up for him. Pate is in Westport; Brown's whereabouts are unknown.

September 20th. We nooned to-day at 110 Creek. The trail is as smooth and as well-worn as a city street.

September 23rd. Prairie chickens were plentiful along the road yesterday. We reached Council Grove, the last outpost of civilization. Two hundred Kaw Indians here.

September 24th. We drove to Elm Creek, where we find a few scattering cottonwoods; all is prairie about here.

September 25th. We rolled over a hard, smooth road to Lost Spring. Our only fuel was buffalo chips. A wagon train from Santa Fe passed.

September 26th. Camped on Cottonwood Creek where we find fine bottoms and considerable timber. Owing to dissensions the members of two wagons unloaded their contents and divided up by lot. Men show their inside character out here where there are none of the restraints of civilization. We elected John Price captain of the train. The comet has been very brilliant for the last two evenings; it stretches clear across the Western sky. The great firebrand and the glittering stars make night seem enchantment and this enchanted land. The night watch passes quickly by as we gaze at the flaming wonder in the heavens and watch, meanwhile, for the sneaking savage in the grass, for the twang of the bow and the silent, death-dealing arrow.

September 28th. We passed Hole-in-the-Prairie and Little Turkey yesterday and camped five miles west of Big Turkey where we found some water in a buffalo wallow.

September 30th. Drove to Cow Creek and camped. Caught some fish in this stream. The country well watered and grass luxuriant. Buffalo and their attendants, big white wolves, very plentiful. We cut buffalo meat into strips and hang them alongside the wagon to dry. We shoot much at prairie dogs but none of the party has yet been able to get

Freight wagons parked at Buffalo Bill's Well, Cow Creek Crossing, Rice County, Kansas, in the 1860s—one of the earliest known photographs of the Santa Fe Trail (courtesy Museum of New Mexico, negative 8285)

---

one. At the flash of the rifle they drop into their holes and disappear. Today, while crawling along a slight depression in the prairie to get inside the fringe of bulls which are always surrounding a herd of buffalo, I heard a sudden rattle just where I was about to put down my hand, and came face-to-face with a rattle-snake coiled for business. In my eagerness to stalk the buffalo I had not noticed him. I was thrilled as with an electric shock and, bounding to my feet, I placed my gun against the snake and blew him to pieces. It was an ungracious act on my part after he had given me fair warning, but I had but one thought in my mind and that was to kill that snake, and I was satisfied to see my cows, one of which I had selected for my meat, go lumbering off over the plain. In the silence of the wilderness with camp made, guards set and the boys gathered around the fires inside the corral, the blue dome above, the flickering lights on the wagon covers and on our bronzed faces, the stage is set for oratory, song and jest. Into the arena struts handsome Jim Winchester, from Virginia, with majestic strides. With fiery speech he thrills his audience. He gives us "Macbeth's Soliloquy" and then retires to his buffalo chip fire amid the plaudits of the whole corral. Big Bill Brannon, from Missouri, in the vernacular of the border tells of stirring events, "Whar' I come from." Dainty Hamp. Boone, of Westport, relates the adventures and "Injun" fights of his ancestors from "Kaintucky" to Missouri, from Daniel Boone to himself. He gives us "Logan's Lament" and, in lurid colors, pictures the wrongs of the "Poor Indian." Bird Martin, of Charlestown, South Carolina, sings the songs of the black slaves of his section and dances the "juba." Red Head Smith, after listening to several repetitions of Clay's speech in Louisville, when he was threatened by the Know Nothings, "Go tell your secret conclave of midnight assassins that Cassius M. Clay knows his rights, and knowing dares maintain them," mounting a wagon tongue and shouted, "Go tell your secret conclave of midnight assassins that Cassius M. Clay knows his rights and no one dare maintain them." His amendment was adopted with tumultuous applause, but he never knew why the camp went wild when he spoke his piece.[8]

October 1st. We strike the big bend of the Arkansas. Good timber and grass here. A Santa Fe train passes. Camped at Walnut Creek. Bill Allison, a one-armed plainsman, has a stockade here and trades with the Indians.[9]

October 2nd. Being on morning watch I saw at dawn large numbers of buffalo near. I started out alone to get a cow or a calf. The country was level and afforded no cover and I was unable to get a shot, but seeing a valley to the left I made for it. Presently five bulls came feeding up the slope. Lying flat on the ground I got a shot at one that exposed his side. The shot revealed my whereabouts and instantly the tufted tails of the whole band were in the air. Bellowing and

[8] Cassius M. Clay helped establish an antislavery community in Kentucky which operated a school for the education of both white and black children. A mob, among whom were members of the American Political party, also called the Know Nothings, broke up the community and forced its leaders to flee the state under threat of death.

[9] William Allison and Francis Boothe established a trading post and stage depot on Walnut Creek in 1855. At the time it was regarded as "the first attempt at building by citizens made west of Council Grove" (Ray S. Schultz, "Allison's Ranch," *Kansas Anthropological Association Newsletter* 15 [Dec., 1969]: 2–3). See also Louise Barry, "The Ranch at Walnut Creek Crossing," *Kansas Historical Quarterly* 37 (Summer 1971): 121–47.

pawing the dust they advanced, their wicked eyes glittering through the matted hair of their foreheads. Loading as best I could without getting to my feet, I fired again and then jumped up and waved my hat and rifle and yelled like a Comanche hoping to stampede them. But they seemed less disposed to stampede than I did; I momentarily expected them to charge. I had found five more buffalo than I wanted. At last one of them wheeled, ran back a short way and lay down; the others turned, went back to their wounded companion, again faced my way, and remained with him for a few minutes, ran back at me again, then turned again and clumsily galloped off down the slope into the valley. Approaching the wounded bull I fired at his forehead, but at the flash he was on his feet, in an instant and I realized that I had a mad buffalo on my trail. I ran toward the train whose dust I could see a long way off. After a close chase for some distance the bull slowed down, spread his fore feet apart and sank to the ground. I then shot him once more under the horns, cut out his tongue and made for the wagons. We nooned today near Pawnee Rock—so named because of the fact that a band of Pawnees surprised some Cheyennes near here and "lifted their hair." Buffalo crossed our trail in such numbers that we had to corral the train to keep from being run over.

October 3rd. Drove over a level country all the forenoon. On both sides of our train, as far as the eye could reach, hordes of buffalo were grazing. It was a peaceful, pastoral scene, except for an occasional fight between buffalo bulls.

October 4th. One of our cattle died last night while a guard was lying in his lee to escape a piercing wind.

October 5th. Our preacher left us today, joined a passing Santa Fe train. This man had been a revivalist in Kansas City and has been drunk ever since we left the border.

October 6th. A cold north wind. Laid by to search for Dr. Woodruff, who has been lost among the sand-hills since yesterday.[10]

[10]This is the first and only mention of Dr. Woodruff's being in the party; he otherwise remains unidentified.

October 7th. A heavy frost last night. Buffalo plenty. Nooned at the ruins of old Fort Atkinson which was once besieged and nearly taken by combined tribes of Indians and was saved by the strategy of Bill Bent who fortunately arrived with his wagon train and camped near by. Taking advantage of the Indians' fondness for sugar he, at the critical moment, after he had sworn at them roundly in French and English and several Indian tongues, diverted them and gained time by breaking open a barrel of sugar and doling out a lump at a time as each Indian filed past his train. The adobe walls remaining are about four feet high.[11]

October 9th. Today the Santa Fe Trail crosses the Arkansas to the south while we continue up the north side. A violent thunder storm struck us this afternoon compelling a hasty camp on a bleak hillside.

October 10th. The storm raged all night. A mule died. Cattle jumped the corral in spite of all our efforts to prevent them and ran into the timber along the river. A fine morning; hunted up the cattle and moved up.

October 11th. While in camp at noon today a large band of Kiowas and Arapahoes came scurrying down the river banks on both sides, going on a buffalo hunt. They swarmed into our corral and insisted that we feed them as toll for passing through their lands. As we saw that they would eat us out of house and home we hurriedly hitched up and drove on. They were sullen and threatening because we would not continue feeding them. All the Indians met lately predict a hard winter on account of the comet. They express themselves quite understandingly to us by the sign language, motioning to us and then pointing to the east whence we came, then to the west where we were going, shrugging their shoulders and pulling their blankets close around them, laying their heads to one side and closing their eyes, is the Indian way of telling us that we white men have come

[11] Fort Atkinson, named for Col. Henry Atkinson, Sixth United States Infantry, was established in 1850 on the left bank of the Arkansas about two miles west of present Dodge City. Although Kellogg says it was constructed of adobe, it was in fact made of sod and, thus, was popularly known as Fort Sod or Fort Sodom. It was abandoned by the army in 1854 (Robert W. Frazer, *Forts of the West* [Norman: University of Oklahoma Press, 1965], pp. 50–51). Bill Bent was William Bent, noted trader and one of the founders of Bent's Old Fort.

from under the sun where it is warm and are going to the mountains where it is cold; and that the malign influence of the comet will be the death of us. The Indian on his pony, clad in breech clout and moccasins, his copper-colored skin glistening in the sun, his head shaved except for a scalp-lock from which dangles an eagle feather, his face painted, riding up to the train with spear and shield of buffalo hide, sitting his horse like a statue, straight as an arrow and as haughty as a the Devil, he is the chief of wonders of this strange land. We trade sugar or coffee for buffalo robes. Pointing to the sugar or coffee, holding up a tin cup and extending five fingers and pointing to the robe is an offer of five cups of sugar or coffee for the robe. If accepted the Indian says, "How, how." The man with the biggest thumb then measures out the required number of cups keeping his thumb inside the cup as he measures. We calculate that one cup in five is gained by the thumb expedient. On the other hand the wily Indian palms off on us his poorest robes. We have been able to get but few good ones. As so many of us want to buy his best robes the Indian decided to keep them. When an Indian shakes your hand he answers your "How are you?" with a deep, gutteral "How." If he accepts your offer for barter he shows his willingness to deal by an emphatic "How, how." Before learning this we held out our cup of sugar and pointed to a robe, asking the Indian "How much?" The Indian repeated "How much?" in a louder tone. He meant that he understood we wanted to trade and that he was willing. I imagine that when the first white man met an Indian he said "How do you do?" The Indian appropriated the first word and afterward used it as a salutation and as a sign of approval. The word "How" seems to be in general use among all the tribes we meet.

October 12th. Two Indians followed and camped with us. During the night there came a yell in the woods along the river at the sound of which they jumped from the tent and ran out into the darkness. We doubled the guard till morning.

October 15th. We reached big timber. Passed several Arapahoe villages. These were located in wooded bends of the river where wood, water and grass are at hand. One which we passed today occupied a most picturesque spot, its location could not have been better chosen by an artist. The tall skin lodges were irregularly scattered over a snug stretch of river bottom, surrounded on three sides by a fine forest of timber and brush with an occasional glimpse of the river showing through the trees. Smoke curled up lazily from between the lodge poles; groups of Indians were squatted on the ground in the sun and the squaws were busy with the various camp duties. The only unfriendliness shown us was by a lot of wolfish-looking dogs. We saw dozens of naked children mounted on ponies, sometimes two or three on a pony; the children rode alongside our wagon train showing the same interest in us as the white boys in the States would show in a circus coming to town.

October 16th. We reached Bent's Fort, where we lay over.[12] This fort is built of rock and stands on a point overlooking the river; a large camp of Cheyennes is near by. Bent's wife, who is a Cheyenne, his son Charley, and his daughter Mollie, are here. Three of our party, myself among the number, had known Mollie Bent in the States and had danced with her in Kansas City; but although we were in and out of the fort all day and once in the very room where she sat with her mother, she paid no attention to us. Mollie was dressed like a white woman but her mother wore the blanket. Bent would stand in the gateway of the fort for hours at a time oblivious to his surroundings, stolid as an Indian.

October 19th. After driving over stony roads for the past few days, we reach the ruins of Bent's old adobe fort.[13] Resting here today we find the woods full of wild grapes and deer. We have seen no buffalo since leaving the crossing of the Arkansas and no prairie chickens since leaving Council Grove.

October 22nd. The Spanish Peaks are dimly seen in the west. Ice formed an inch thick last night. Three Arapahoes came into camp from a scout in the Ute country and reported having seen gold-dust on the riffles in the river. Several of us took our pans and rushed into the shallow stream to prospect. The glittering yellow and white particles all ran over the pan with the water; it glittered but was not

[12] This was Bent's New Fort, built by William in 1853 about eight miles upriver from present Lamar, Colorado.
[13] Bent's Old Fort, abandoned by William in 1849, lies between Las Animas and La Junta, Colorado, and is now a restored National Historic Site.

gold, but mica. The great blue barrier is growing ahead of us, the long-looked for mountain chain.

October 23rd. Some Cherokee Indians passed, returning to Georgia.

October 24th. Charley Otterby and a squaw passed going to their ranch on the Huerfano.[14] Reached the mouth of Fontaine Que Bouille, or Boiling Fountain Creek, a stream coming from the north and entering the Arkansas here. Concealed among a lot of rocks on the point over which our trail passes was an Arapahoe, watching the country around for the signs of Utes. From daylight to dark an Indian lookout is always stationed here by whatever tribe happens to have possession. We find a number of adobe houses and a few log huts, all empty save one. This place was once a Mexican pueblo and the ruins of their adobe fort still stands on the west side of the creek. The Utes took the fort, massacred its occupants and wiped out the settlement. We find George McDougal living here with a Mexican woman and several greasers.[15]

McDougal took us to his smokehouse which was filled with antelope hams and invited us to help ourselves; he gave us much useful information concerning the country, the route and the Indians. Said we should find plenty of antelope at Jim's camp, and he advised us to supply ourselves there.[16] Drove up the creek five miles and camped.

October 25th. A severe storm struck us last night; the guard crept into the wagons and went to sleep. In the morning the impress of many pony tracks around the corral gave mute evidence that we had been visited by Indians during the night. While at breakfast McDougal rode up to tell us that a band of Utes had been at his camp at daylight and had boasted that they had caught our camp asleep and

[14] Trapper Charles Autobees settled at the mouth of the Huerfano River in 1853 and ranched there until his death in 1882. The Huerfano enters the Arkansas about twenty miles east of Pueblo, Colo. (Janet Lecompte, "Charles Autobees," in Hafen, *Mountain Men and the Fur Trade,* 4:37).

[15] The early history of Pueblo is related by Janet Lecompte in *Pueblo, Hardscrabble, Greenhorn: The Upper Arkansas, 1832–1856* (Norman: University of Oklahoma Press, 1978). Therein (p. 234) the author describes George McDougal as "the dissipated brother of a later senator from California."

[16] Jim's, or Jimmy's, Camp was a settlement ten miles east of modern Colorado Springs, located on the trail between Pueblo and Denver.

could have captured our trains and killed us all. He warned us that if we traveled in so careless a manner we would get wiped out.

October 26th. Continuing up Fountain Creek we kill many wild turkeys.

7. Henry Smith's Recollections, 1863

For more than a century the great glowing West exerted its magnetic pull, luring onward the venturesome and daring among American youth. In the wilderness beyond the line of settlement could be found challenge and adventure, vast profits, and sometimes death. The Santa Fe Trail, richly endowed with romance and the salt of danger, witnessed its share of youngsters following the deeply scored wagon tracks southwestward to the storied land of New Mexico.

Kit Carson was barely seventeen when he fled his apprenticeship in a saddler's shop at Franklin, Missouri, and joined a caravan for Santa Fe. It was the beginning of a journey that eventually would lead him into the history books. Another seventeen year old who took to the trail in search of excitement was Louis Hector Garrard. The record of his experiences in 1846 and 1847, incorporated in Wah-to-yah and the Taos Trail, *stands as a superlative contribution to the literature of western travel.[1] Then there were Susan Magoffin, who went to Santa Fe in 1846 as a new bride of eighteen, and Marian Sloan [Russell], who left Fort Leavenworth in 1852, at the age of seven, for the first of many Santa Fe Trail crossings with her mother and brother.[2]*

Henry Smith, whose recollections are presented here, was living in eastern Kansas as a lad of sixteen when he responded to the call of his "pioneer blood," as he himself phrased it. During the

[1] Lewis H. Garrard, *Wah-to-yah and the Taos Trail* (Norman: University of Oklahoma Press, 1955).

[2] Stella M. Drumm, ed., *Down the Santa Fe Trail and into Mexico: The Diary of Susan Shelby Magoffin, 1846–1847* (New Haven, Conn.: Yale University Press, 1962); and Garnet M. Brayer, ed., *Land of Enchantment: Memoirs of Marian Russell along the Santa Fe Trail* (Evanston, Ill.: Branding Iron Press, 1954).

dark days of the Civil War, the opportunity arose to hire on with a governmental supply train, bound for Fort Union, New Mexico; and in spite of promised perils and hardships, he seized it with enthusiasm. The trip, as the account makes clear, transformed a pale young store clerk in a paper collar into a sturdy individual "seasoned to outdoor life, bronzed and strong."

Smith's recollections, while lacking both the length and depth of, say, the Garrard or Magoffin narratives, do provide a useful and significant view of one youth's encounter with daily living on the Santa Fe Trail. Evidently they were written late in life, after the author had taken up residence in Kansas City. On March 6, 1907, his daughter, Mrs. M. T. Burwell, Jr., read the recollections before the Athena Ladies Club of Goodland, Kansas. Shortly after that they were privately printed in a twenty-page pamphlet with colored wrappers, which is now exceedingly rare.[3] The republication here includes all of Smith's actual experiences but deletes several introductory and concluding paragraphs that treat in the broadest terms the general history of the trail.

Kansas had few settlements west of a line running north and south through Topeka. Indian troubles and long and difficult journeys compelled the government to transport its supplies to the western borders, and Fort Leavenworth was its principal depot of supplies for the Southwest. The government had been able later to make contracts for transportation, but up to the year 1863, it still kept a few trains for that purpose. The train that I became attached to was their last undertaking, as subsequently transportation was by contract.

Heredity and Environment

A miller with his family came to and settled in Missouri in 1816. He made the journey from New York on the Ohio and Mississippi

[3] For a bibliographical description of the pamphlet see Jack D. Rittenhouse, *The Santa Fe Trail: A Historical Bibliography* (Albuquerque: University of New Mexico Press, 1971), p. 194. A photocopy was supplied to me by the Kansas State Historical Society, Topeka, whose assistance is gratefully acknowledged.

Rivers by flatboat. In 1822 he built a mill and for many years operated it in Clay County, one mile from the state line, and twenty miles north of the Kaw's mouth. The evolution from "Smith's Mill" to Smithville was not difficult and that was the place of my birth and home until the Spring of 1862. It was at that time that my father, a Union man, impelled by the perils of the Civil War, moved to Grasshopper—now Valley Falls, Kansas. He took with us to that place ten negro slaves, and gave them freedom many months before President Lincoln issued his Emancipation Proclamation. I was then sixteen years old, and became a clerk in my father's store. He furnished supplies to the Government employees who were wintering and tending cattle in that vicinity. In this way I came to know and form a friendship for the wagon master, Henderson, in charge of the men. He gave and I accepted an invitation to make the trip "across the plains" the following summer. Of pioneer blood and environments, I long desired such adventure. But how was I to go? I did not have the strength to lift the heavy yokes and yoke the oxen, nor did I have the age and experience to drive and conduct a heavily loaded wagon drawn by a team of four yoke of cattle. Indeed the Government would not have accepted me for such a service. But my friend, Henderson, agreed to manage the matter for me, and he did. So, early in the following June, under arrangement with Mr. Henderson, I reported at Fort Leavenworth for service. Slender, not robust, and bleached by indoor life, with the appearance of a country store clerk, still wearing a paper collar—the usual thing at that time—I entered upon camp life, and of course, attracted the attention of the crew and of Levi Wilson, then in charge of the outfitting of Government trains. The men made remarks about me, Mr. Wilson looked at me doubtingly, and said I would not need my paper collars on that trip.

We had thirty wagons, four yoke of oxen with a driver for each wagon, a wagon master and his assistant, and two boys to drive the extra oxen and twenty unbroken young mules and a bell mare for the mules to follow. All this train and its freight were to be taken and turned over to the commandant at Fort Union in New Mexico. The wagon master, his assistant and the two boys (I was one of the boys) were provided with mules to ride. We were given the regular army rations of bacon, flour, sugar, coffee and dessicated, or dried, potatoes and vegetables. These potatoes and vegetables were unpalatable and uneaten. There were no canned goods in those days.

A heavy wagon of the type used for freight on the Santa Fe Trail

Our kitchen and tableware consisted of a frying pan, oven, a coffee pot, and tin plates and cups. When beyond the settlements our cooking fuel was dried "buffalo chips." We were armed, each one of us, with an old muzzle loading musket with ammunition. Our load was about seven thousand pounds of bacon to each wagon. Nearly all of the train crew were from the State of Missouri, finding in this occupation a refuge from the conflicts of Civil War. I heard very little political talk, but all I did hear showed a sympathy from the men for the Southern people. My boy companion was from Rolla, Missouri, and even I was a Missouri refugee.

The Outward Trip

Our start was in the rain, on muddy roads, with men and cattle unused to work, and it was therefore most difficult. With great effort we reached Salt Creek Valley the first day, still in sight of the fort. We made slow progress on the "Military Road" to Easton, Winchester, Osawke, Muddy and Soldier Creek to Topeka. Winchester was a short ride from my home, so when we reached that place Henderson and I made a visit there. The Kaw River was not bridged at Topeka where we crossed it; so that the cattle and mules swam it and the wagons were taken over on a hand ferry boat. The "Doniphan Expedition" had crossed the Kaw at the mouth of Bull Creek, only about thirty miles from the Kaw mouth, and reached the regular Santa Fe Trail at the "Narrows," fifty miles west of Westport.[4] From Topeka we proceeded southward to the regular Santa Fe Trail a hundred miles from Westport at a point that is now Burlingame, Kansas. We then proceded westerly to Council Grove, the last village or settlement on the Trail. Then to Diamond Springs, Cottonwood, Turkey Creek, Little Arkansas, Cow Creek to the Big Bend of the Arkansas River, where we found a village of more than one thousand Indians that made us anxious and uneasy, as we did not know their disposition toward us. These Indians were Kiowas, and their great chief was Satanta, who had the reputation of being troublesome and vicious.[5] Their boys would shoot arrows into our cattle while grazing, and annoyed us in many ways. Indians and buffaloes became very numerous and continued so for many days. We escaped injury, but the following Fall the Indians went on the war path and committed many atrocities and depredations.

It was at Cow Creek, that Chauvey, a New Mexican trader, in 1843, was robbed and murdered by a marauding party of fifteen headed by Captain John McDaniel. Their booty was ten thousand dollars in gold bullion. The captain and one of the gang were tried in the Federal Court at St. Louis, convicted and hung. Most of the others suffered imprisonment for the crime.[6]

[4] Col. Alexander W. Doniphan commanded the First Regiment Missouri Mounted Volunteers, a part of the Army of the West that marched over the Santa Fe Trail in 1846 at the outbreak of the Mexican War. John T. Hughes, official chronicler of the expedition, writes: "There was no road, nor even a path leading from Fort Leavenworth into the regular Santa Fe trail. The army therefore steered its course south-westerly, with the view of intersecting the main Santa Fe trace, at or near the Narrows, sixty-five miles west of Independence" (*Doniphan's Expedition* [Cincinnati, Ohio: U. P. James, 1847], p. 141).

[5] On the conduct of Satanta during the 1860s see Leo E. Oliva, *Soldiers on the Santa Fe Trail* (Norman: University of Oklahoma Press, 1967), pp. 182–84.

[6] The New Mexican trader was Antonio José Chávez. His slaying in April, 1843, by "land pirates" west of the Little Arkansas crossing threw the Missouri-Kansas frontier into an uproar, since it threatened to disrupt the valuable international trade with Santa Fe and Chihuahua City. Jarvis Creek (a corruption of Chávez) lies southeast of Lyons, Kansas, its name commemorating that tragic incident.

By the time we reached the Arkansas Valley the working condition of the train was improved. The men had become acquainted with each other and learned their duties, the cattle were used to their work, and the loose stock to travel. The loose stock was known as the "cavallard," and its drivers broke all the mules to the saddle before we reached Fort Union.[7] The cattle had only the grass on the way to live upon, so that it was very important that each camp should be at a place, where there was plenty of grass and water. Such places were known to or ascertained by the wagon master or his assistant. At every camp the train was formed into a corral, that is, the wagons were driven up close together so as to form a circle, including about one acre with a twenty foot opening in front and behind. In this enclosure we cooked, ate, slept and yoked the cattle. Our drives, to avoid the heat of the day, were early in the morning and in the afternoon, and were about eight miles each, or sixteen miles daily. During the middle of the day and at night the stock grazed under the watch of two men. We had messes of about eight men each, who selected, of their number, one as a cook, exempt from watch duty. I was of the mess of the wagon master and his assistant. There was plenty of game, and as often as we cared to, we dined on jack rabbit, antelope, elk and buffalo that herded on our way in thousands. On account of the purity of the air, fresh meat did not spoil, and we kept it as long as desired. Graves were frequent along the route, and their suggestions were not pleasant to a boy away from home under such wild conditions. Tradition usually connected the occupants of the graves with tragedies. Coyotes were reputed to despoil the graves, and their gruesome cries nightly made me believe that it was true. Sage brush, cactus, buffalo and grama grasses, chameleons, prairie lizards, horned frogs and prairie dog villages belonged to the country and were new and interesting to me.

As I recollect, there was a monthly mail route on the Trail, but I do not remember of seeing more than one or two stages or stage stations.

[7] *Cavallard* or *cavvyard*, often shortened to *cavvy*, was derived from the Spanish *caballada*, meaning a herd of saddle horses. On the Santa Fe Trail the term was expanded to include draft stock, such as mules and oxen.

The Raton Route

At a point where now is Dodge City the regular Santa Fe Trail crossed the Arkansas River and was known to us as the "Cimarron Route." The Government required us to take the Raton Route lest our train be captured by Confederates. The Confederates, in 1862, came out of Texas and took and occupied Santa Fe. They had a small fight with the Federals near Fort Union, so we continued on the north side of the river, by Fort Lyon to "Bent's Old Fort," where we crossed. We were now really in the desert. It was the short grass country. We could plainly see the mountains, Pike's Peak, the Spanish Peaks and Long's Peak more than a hundred miles but apparently not more than ten miles distant. Our longest and hardest drive, on the entire trip, was from the river to Iron Springs, which we reached at midnight, man and stock in an exhausted condition.[8] The water was black as ink and unfit for use, so early next morning we started on a long drive to the base of the Raton Mountains, and finally reached the Pugatoire, a mountain stream of remarkably pure limpid and cold water that we could well appreciate. After a day's rest we traveled up that stream by Gray's mill, the Mexican village of Trinidad and over Dick Wootten's toll road to the Raton summit.[9] The ascent of the Raton pass was slow and difficult, with our heavily loaded wagons, so that we were several days traveling a few miles. This gave opportunity for me to enjoy the wooded forests, and the fresh air of these splendid mountains.

It was upon this toll road that our train passed by another Government train returning east. Pat Sherman was wagon master. He was afterwards for many years marshal of Topeka, Kansas. We proceeded more rapidly down from the Raton summit past the two million acre "Maxwell Land Grant," and arrived at Fort Union, the end of our journey.

[8] The Missouri Stage Company built a station for its coaches at Iron Spring early in 1861.

[9] Gray's Mill, or Gray's Ranch, was founded in 1861 by Kentuckian James S. Gray. That same year it became a designated stage stop. Richens ("Uncle Dick") Lacy Wootton, famed mountain man and Santa Fe Trail freighter, opened his celebrated toll road over Raton Pass in 1865, two years after Henry Smith traveled that way.

The Return Trip

After the property in our charge was turned over to Fort Union, we were notified that such of us as desired could proceed farther with a train to Albuquerque, that such as did not desire to go would be furnished a wagon and three yoke of oxen to attend them on their return to Fort Leavenworth. It was not left to me to decide what I should do, as Henderson informed me that we would return. He had promised my mother that he would bring me back home in safety. He retained his mule to ride. After a few days we set our faces eastward with the team carrying our blankets and cooking utensils. About one-half of the men returned with us. There was no reason why we should not take the Cimarron Route, and as it was shorter and some of us had not seen it, we returned that way. We found little water or grass on the route, and the last drive before reaching the Cimarron Crossing, a sixty mile drive, was entirely without water, only the little we carried in a couple of kegs swung under the wagon. The cattle had none. This dry stretch was known to us as the "hornada," from the Spanish "jornada del muerto," journey of death. Mirages of beautiful lakes of water were frequent on this route.

Our journey eastward along the bottom of the Arkansas was slow and leisurely, traveling about ten or twelve miles in the morning and the same distance in the afternoon daily. I had become seasoned to outdoor life by living, eating and sleeping in the open air for nearly three months, was bronzed and strong, no longer the frail boy, the pale faced clerk with a paper collar. These walks were to me a pleasure and a delight.

Home Again

Our last camp was near Topeka, twenty-five miles from my home. Early in the morning I left the camp, walking most of the time, riding occasionally in a passing wagon, and reached home at sundown, unexpected by the family. The clothes I wore consisted of a woolen shirt, a very dirty pair of pants, a hat and a pair of Indian moccasins, all of the value, if new, of less than three dollars. The clothes were of such infection and condition as not to be permissible in the house, so were thrown away at once, and a much needed bath taken.

A few days later, I went to Fort Leavenworth to receive my pay of about one hundred dollars, at thirty dollars per month. The men had dispersed and gone; with one exception I never saw them afterwards. My friend Henderson continued in the Government employ and the following year was killed by Confederates in the vicinity of Fort Scott, Kansas.

The period of my absence was full of great events to the Nation, of which I knew absolutely nothing until my return. The great battle of Gettysburg had been fought, Vicksburg had been taken and Lawrence had been sacked and burned by Quantrell.

Ten days after my return I was a student in the University of Michigan. The trip gave me renewed vitality and strength, and gave me an information and experience that has been of value in my subsequent life. Parts of this story, as I have now told it, I often told to my school mates, relating in greater detail the events of the trip, then fresh in my mind, to their and my delectation and entertainment.

8. Ernestine Franke
Huning's Diary, 1863

Women were scarce on the Santa Fe Trail. Indeed, during the first twenty-five years that the route was in use, probably fewer than a dozen women crossed it, and they were mainly female relatives of Mexican businessmen traveling east. Susan Magoffin, the wife of trader Samuel Magoffin, accompanied her husband to New Mexico in 1846, a full quarter-century after the Santa Fe Trail was opened. And she claims in her published journal to have been the first American lady to have made such a trip.[1] The reason was that up to that date the road from Missouri to the Southwest had been traveled largely by merchants and teamsters who, once their goods were delivered, returned home at the end of the summer's trading season. There was little cause, therefore, for them to take their women on a short-term prairie journey that usually was fraught with peril.

The situation changed in 1846, after an American army had seized New Mexico (in the first year of the Mexican War), bringing the far end of the Santa Fe Trail into the hands of the United States. Merchants from Missouri and other states began to settle in the new territory, taking with them their wives and families. And in succeeding years, other sorts of women also rode the trail to New Mexico— nuns and wives of Protestant missionaries, wives of soldiers newly posted to the Southwest, and a few ladies who accompanied their menfolk on their way to the gold fields in the California rush of '49 and the Colorado rush of '59. Still, the numbers of women remained small—nothing like the thousands who swarmed west on the Oregon

[1] Drumm, *Down the Santa Fe Trail*, p. 102. For a bibliographical listing of women's trail diaries and memoirs see Marc Simmons, "Women on the Santa Fe Trail," *New Mexico Historical Review* 61 (July, 1986): 233–43.

Reproduction of a tintype of Franz Huning,
made in his Santa Fe Trail trading days
(courtesy Mrs. Alexander Caemmerer, Jr.)

and Mormon emigrant routes—and as a consequence, diaries and journals that provide a feminine perspective of the Santa Fe Trail are rare.

Among that select group is the account of Ernestine Franke Huning, who went over the trail with her new husband, Franz Huning, to his home in Albuquerque in late spring of 1863. Franz had immigrated from Germany to the United States in 1849 as a youth of twenty-two. He went first to St. Louis, which boasted a large German colony; then in search of frontier adventure, he moved on to Fort Leavenworth, where he joined a Santa Fe–bound train as a bull whacker. Eventually he settled in Albuquerque, fifty miles down the Rio Grande from Santa Fe, developed a prosperous mercantile firm, and proceeded to make yearly trips with his own freight caravan to the wholesalers in Kansas City and St. Louis.

During the winter of 1862/63, Franz Huning paid a brief visit to his relatives in Germany. Returning by steamer, he landed in New York in July, 1863, just a few days after the Battle of Gettysburg. In the face of difficulties associated with wartime, he made his way back to St. Louis and there purchased the goods that he would need in his Albuquerque store for the coming year. In the German community he also found a wife.[2] According to his grandson, the distinguished novelist Harvey Fergusson, "On his way home [Franz] met in St. Louis a plump, good-humored, flaxen-haired girl from Bavaria, promptly married her and took her West, together with ten canary birds she refused to leave behind."[3]

These are the circumstances that led Ernestine Huning to be on the Santa Fe Trail while Civil War raged in the East. As her diary plainly shows, the journey was made in relative comfort and safety. During the first few days she dined on goose breast and truffles, prepared by her husband's cook; and even later, when crossing the dreaded Jornada, there were oranges and wines to quench her thirst. All that was missing was cake, she notes. Aside from a close call involving Indians and Confederate raiders along the Cimarron Cutoff, nothing disturbed the Hunings' peaceful trip over the plains. In his own separate journal, Franz wrote: "We arrived home in good

---

[2] Franz's account of these events appears in Lina Fergusson Browne, ed., *Trader on the Santa Fe Trail: The Memoirs of Franz Huning* (Albuquerque, N.Mex.: Calvin Horn Publisher, 1973), pp. 72–73.

[3] Harvey Fergusson, *Home in the West* (New York: Duell, Sloan Pearce, 1944), p. 37.

Ernestine Franke Huning (courtesy Mrs. Alexander Caemmerer, Jr.)

---

shape."[4] *Ernestine ends her account with an entry of May 30, in which the party reaches Las Vegas, the first major New Mexican town to be encountered on the trail.*

The diary depicts a pleasant jaunt on the trail, marred by little in the way of inclement weather or threats to life and property, which was scarcely representative of travel to Santa Fe in the 1860s. Ernestine Huning apparently had a streak of good luck. In sharp contrast, her mother and younger brother, as they were coming West four years later in one of Franz's wagon trains, were massacred near Plum Buttes in central Kansas. Details of that tragic episode are related below in Document 11.[5]

[4] Browne, *Trader on the Santa Fe Trail*, p. 73.
[5] Ernestine's diary, originally written in German, was translated by her eldest daughter, Clara Huning Fergusson. A typescript is preserved among the Huning-Fergusson Papers, Special Collections, Zimmerman Library, University of New

April 4: The fourth of April we left St. Louis, Mo., went by boat to Hannibal, from there by rail to St. Joseph, then to Weston, and there took the boat again as far as Leavenworth. There we had to wait six days before going out to camp, but our goods not having arrived we went to a hotel near there. The weather was disagreeable and cold, later on very windy.

April 15: The third day of being in camp which did not prove as disagreeable as we feared. The beans and ham taste very good in the open, the air giving us a good appetite. Yesterday we had goose breast and truffles, but I do not think they tasted better than our regular fare. The only disagreeable part so far has been the everlasting waiting on our trunks, especially as we are having beautiful moonshine and could be traveling.

April 19: We are still waiting for the rest of the goods, my husband getting impatient at the delay. However, all of the party are well. Our cook, a colored woman, entertains us sometimes by telling our fortunes.

April 20: Our goods finally arrived, but not my husband who had gone to hurry them up. That evening we had a wonderful thunderstorm, which however only lasted half an hour.

April 21: We are finally ready to go on, everything is in order to make an early start next day.

April 22: We traveled about twenty five miles, then made camp. The day being disagreeable, we remained in our ambulance.

April 23: We passed through the prettiest part of Kansas. We have plenty of company and enjoy ourselves. Mr. Funke, Mr. Frenger, and an American, Mr. Louis, sing for us sometimes so we are always merry.[6] We are getting used to our way of living, and have as

Mexico, Albuquerque. The complete document is here published for the first time, by permission. It should be noted, however, that brief excerpts were included in Browne, *Trader on the Santa Fe Trail,* pp. 73–75.

[6] Franz, in his memoirs, states that his party consisted of six men and two teams (Browne, *Trader on the Santa Fe Trail,* p. 72). The three individuals mentioned by Ernestine are not identified, but Funke and Frenger were probably recent German immigrants.

many comforts as possible. We have china dishes, camp chairs, and a table, so we dine quite well.

April 24: We crossed the Kansas River and passed through Topeka, a small not pretty town.

April 25: We started about five o'clock in the morning, had lovely weather, and passed through beautiful country, camping near a creek. Our ten canaries, which we brought from St. Louis, sing a good deal, the traveling seems to agree with them. Also Nero, our dog, is behaving well, being satisfied to lie in the wagon. Although the day was rather warm, the evening is cool. We had rather a disagreeable experience later. We were still sitting around talking when it was noticed that the animals were restless, and someone reported having seen two men on horseback. All the men went for their guns to reconnoiter. However, no riders were seen, but two mules were missing.

April 26: We started rather late, doing the best we could without the two mules, and finally reached Wilmington.[7] From there several men went back to look for the mules. As they were branded they thought the thieves would let them go, and sure enough they got back with them about noon. We started at once, camping for the night near a creek.

April 28: We started early, went six miles, and then stopped for breakfast. Almost every place we stopped there were several houses, and the people came and admired our birds and our traveling arrangements.

April 29: We started early, went as far as Council Grove, and saw the first Indians, three men and two women.[8] These are supposed to be of the better class, but they act like children. They lie down on the ground on their stomachs, both men and women, and dress almost

[7] Wilmington, between modern Burlington and Council Grove, lay a few miles north of the main Santa Fe Trail. The Hunings had started over a popular alternate trail from Leavenworth via Topeka that joined the principal route just east of Council Grove.

[8] These no doubt were Kaw Indians, whose agency was located about four miles southeast of Council Grove near the mouth of Big John Creek.

alike. When we were through eating, we gave them food, but they hardly could use a spoon.

May 1: We started early, and it was so lovely after sunrise that we got out and walked awhile. We passed through Diamond Springs, where we saw some houses which had been destroyed during the rebellion. A breakfast of potato salad, ham, and eggs, fresh butter and biscuit and coffee will taste good after our early walk. We are over the worst of the road as it promises to be more level after this, and if the weather is good the rest of the trip will be pleasant. The beer we get tastes good, although it is not St. Louis beer. We had quail for supper, which we enjoyed.

May 3: We traveled quite a distance today. Got water at Little Turkey.

May 4: We met some Indians, and they were all friendly.

May 5: Weather fine. Stopped at Cow Creek to camp. Trees are in leaf and full of blossoms, quite a relief after the dreary desert. We rested here all day to give the mules a chance for a rest too.

May 6: We meet Indians very often now, some have their faces painted. Naturally they have a dark complexion. All are tall, well built. They always beg, but are satisfied when they get something to eat, and go. We saw one of their houses made of branches with a hole in the middle for the smoke to go out, as they cook by making a fire inside. We have seen no buffaloes alive, but many dead lying along the road. Have tried the dried buffalo meat, but do not like it.

May 7: We had a hard thunderstorm lasting a long time. It is a queer sensation to experience a storm out on the open prairie.

May 8: Everything is fresh and lovely, the foliage a beautiful green. We arrived at Fort D[odge]. These will be the last houses we shall see on our trip. Our dog must have gone back to the Fort as we could not find him and had to go on without him. My husband and Mrs. Franz are both sick, which is bad when we can do nothing for them.[9]

---

[9] Mrs. Franz was the sister of E. D. Franz, Huning's business partner in new Mexico. She had accompanied Franz Huning from Europe on the way to join her

May 10: A good day, so we started early and traveled quite a distance, saw quantities of cactus of different kinds. Mr. Louis shot a rabbit which varied our food a bit. We also saw antelope and buffalo, but the men could not shoot any.

May 12: The weather is lovely, and for hours we drove along the Arkansas River and we had green vegetables for dinner, raised right there. Toward evening we had to ford the Arkansas River, and although I am not easily frightened, I must confess that I did not feel very comfortable when we were in the middle, but we got through without trouble.[10] The weather is getting quite warm and I have had little appetite for several days. The worst of our journey is behind us, so I hope we will get over the rest of the way without trouble. We had an early supper and drove for several hours in the evening. I walked beside the wagon and felt better for my exercise.

May 12: The weather is lovely, and we see lots of antelope without being able to shoot one. We met two trains which were loaded with wool. On account of mild weather we drove till ten o'clock at night. We are near Sand Creek, and the view is beautiful, clouds throw shadows on green meadows making a striking contrast, and we can imagine ourselves in a park, though the refreshments are lacking. We can eat some oranges and drink a glass of wine, but the cake we have to imagine.

May 14, 15, 16: Nothing special happened. We met two families from Mexico traveling East where they expect to live. We also met several wagon trains, so it did not seem as if we were far away from civilization.

May 18: It is just as if we were driving through an immense flower garden, the wild flowers are so thick and lovely.

May 19 and 20: We came to a lovely spring called Upper Semer or Casa Depallo. We bought a lamp from some Mexicans. It is a

brother. She probably rode in the ambulance, a common passenger conveyance, with Ernestine and possibly the cook (Browne, *Trader on the Santa Fe Trail,* pp. 68, 72).

[10] This reference seems to refer to what was called the Upper Crossing of the Arkansas near modern Lakin, Kansas. From that point the Santa Fe Trail led across the Jornada to Sand Creek and the Cimarron River.

beautiful camping place, the cliffs look as if they had been hewn into beautiful shapes. I picked some wild gooseberries, which were pretty good when cooked. Another spring is called Cold Spring.[11]

May 22: We got up at four o'clock to get an early start, and at half past six arrived at Cedar Springs.[12] We can see several mountain ranges, called Rabbit Ears and Sierra Grande. We are in the territory of New Mexico now, and the scene is constantly changing: forests, mountains, and plains. We passed five wagons, but saw no people and no mules. But about two miles farther we saw a wagon train, and they explained that the day before twenty to twenty five Indians had attacked a train, and besides $10,000 in gold and fifty mules, had taken what else they could use. Fortunately it belonged to a very rich man who will not miss it. No one was killed, as the wagon master had gone to buy sheep and the men were with him which saved them.

In the afternoon we met a man who had been with the attacked train, and who had to be interpreter as he was an American and the Guerrillas did not understand Spanish. He had to take off his coat because one of the band wanted it. They came two at a time on horseback, well-armed. This is a bad night for us and we wish we were six days farther along, as we do not feel safe at all.[13]

May 23: It rained a good deal during the night, but is lovely today.

May 24: Last night we had a terrible storm, but it is lovely today. Here is a spring with good water called Wet Stone.[14] Here we met

[11] Upper Cimarron Spring, also known as Flag Spring, was located about eight miles northwest of present Boise City, Oklahoma. Four miles beyond it on the trail was Cold Spring.

[12] Cedar Springs is located in the far Oklahoma Panhandle, about five miles east of the New Mexico line. To guard the Santa Fe Trail, Kit Carson established a temporary post, Camp Nichols, near the site in the summer of 1865.

[13] Ernestine's rather confused recital of this incident can be compared with her husband Franz's account, in Browne, *Trader on the Santa Fe Trail*, pp. 72–73: "We arrived at Cedar Springs just late enough to not fall into the hands of some Texans. We found there a mule train camped, with wagon and harness in good shape, but neither men nor mules to be seen. Fresh tracks showed that the mules had been run off in a southerly direction and other tracks proved that the depredation had not been committed by Indians. We saw none of the men of the train, nor did I ever find out whose train it was. If we had reached the place maybe only a few hours sooner, we certainly would have shared the same fate."

[14] Whetstone Creek was a familiar campsite on the trail between the Round Mound and Point of Rocks in northeastern New Mexico.

some herders who gave us a quarter of antelope for some salt. The meat tastes like venison.

May 26 and 27: Good weather. We can see the Mexican mountains covered with snow; the sun shining on them brings them out clearly. We drove through the Colorado River; it was quite narrow.[15] We passed a house where some herders lived.

May 27: Bad weather. We had to travel slowly.

May 28: More rain. I hope they have better weather in St. Louis on account of their fair. I will be glad to arrive at our destination; the rain has delayed us so. We passed a house where the land surrounding it was well cultivated and a large flock of sheep was grazing not far off. The house had a beautiful location between hills in the valley called Santa Clara, where there are a number of nice springs.[16]

May 29: Nice weather. Wooded hills make the scenery attractive; the stream coming down the rocks rushes like a river. This afternoon we have a wonderful view in front of us. As far as we can see are snow-covered mountains which reach into the white clouds, and lower down forests all along the base. We saw a group of houses built by a German who had located there and built so many houses that it looked like a village.[17] We had expected to stop only for water, but the river we had to cross was so high that we had to wait till next day.

May 30: Weather fine. We stopped about five miles from Las Vegas and went to the Hot Springs where we took a room to take some of the baths which are said to be very good.[18] We will stay three days.

[15] The Colorado was the New Mexican name for the Canadian River. The trail crossed it about five miles east of Springer, New Mexico.

[16] Santa Clara Springs, the site of a stage station, lay close to a famous trail landmark, the Wagon Mound.

[17] The German was surely William Kronig, who came over the trail to New Mexico in 1849 and established a large ranch on the Sapello River at La Junta, now Watrous (see Charles Irving Jones, "William Kronig, New Mexico Pioneer," *New Mexico Historical Review* 19 [July, 1944]: 185–224).

[18] The famous Las Vegas Hot Springs were later acquired by the A T & S F Railroad, which built a resort and spa at the site. Today it is the location of the United World College.

The scenery is pretty, mountains covered with trees all around us. I enjoyed the fruit put up here, peaches, berries, and pears.

9. Reminiscences of George E. Vanderwalker, 1864

When the Civil War broke out in 1861, some men who had no interest in the conflict went west in an effort to escape it. But that is not why teenager George E. Vanderwalker headed for the frontier. He was eager to fight for the Union cause; but because of his age and small size, his enlistment was rejected. So, filled with the spirit of adventure, he made his way to Leavenworth, Kansas, and in time was hired as a bull whacker by the firm of Stewart Stemens, which was engaged in freighting military supplies over the Santa Fe Trail. Since the war had caused a shortage of manpower, the company was willing to take on an undersized greenhorn like Vanderwalker.

He had been born on July 10, 1848, in Constantine, Michigan, where he spent his boyhood. Although he had a familiarity with milk cows, suggesting that he was raised on a farm, there was little else in the youth's background that might have prepared him for life on a western trail. When he descended from the stagecoach at Diamond Spring, a campsite west of Council Grove where he was to join his bull outfit, he was completely untutored in the skills of a plainsman.

In his trail reminiscences, Vanderwalker explains the organization of a wagon train, the methods used to break and handle oxen, and the nature of camp life; he also tells of a night stampede by the livestock. Unlike many another party of the period, he and his companions managed to slip through central and western Kansas without encountering hostile Indians.[1]

George Vanderwalker's account lacks the seriousness of tone and the tendency toward dryness that characterize perhaps the

---

[1] George E. Vanderwalker's reminiscences were published in two parts: "The Bull-wacker or Prairie Sailor," *The Trail* 1 (Feb., 1909): 26–28, and "Over the Santa Fe Trail in '64," *The Trail* 2 (June, 1909): 15–18.

majority of contemporary writings about the Santa Fe Trail. Indeed, he enlivens his tale with a pointed sense of humor, although one that is devoid of any measure of subtlety. Trail bibliographer Jack D. Rittenhouse, in fact, notes only one other attempt at a humorous treatment of the subject—a satirical journal of a trip to Santa Fe written in Biblical language and first published in the Missouri Intelligencer *for August 5 and 19, 1825.*[2]

Vanderwalker seems to have been particularly amused when he met, near the summit of Raton Pass, teamsters in the employ of Russell, Majors and Waddell. He mentions that each one had been furnished a Bible by the company, and no doubt he was aware that every man had signed a labor contract, agreeing not to use profane language, get drunk, gamble, treat animals cruelly, or travel on the Sabbath, under penalty of immediate discharge without pay. Notwithstanding, the rocky trail over the pass had proved so vexing that the drovers forgot their obligations and resorted to the strongest of language in trying to hurry up the oxen.

After his caravan's supplies had been delivered to Fort Union, Vanderwalker returned to Leavenworth; from there he made his way home to Michigan. His rugged adventure to the Southwest had both aged and hardened him, with the result that he was now able to join the Eleventh Michigan Infantry. He remained in active service with that unit to the close of the war, being mustered out at Chattanooga, Tennessee.

Later in life he went west again, this time to Colorado, where he engaged in prospecting in the vicinity of Leadville. Afterwards, with his wife and two sons, he settled at the mountain town of Cripple Creek, where he died of heart failure on April 27, 1914.[3]

Part I

Sometime since I read an article giving an account of an anniversary of some "ancient mariners" and others, and of how badly disappointed one of the number was on account of his inability, after a wide search, to procure a pair of oxen, broken to the yoke, to use in

[2] Rittenhouse, *The Santa Fe Trail*, p. 234.

[3] Biographical details have been taken from his obituary, "George E. Vanderwalker," *The Trail* 6 (May, 1914): 28–29.

George E. Vanderwalker (courtesy University of New Mexico)

a parade on the said occasion. I take it his intention being to show the new generation how we "did things" in the early days. He certainly showed his good judgment in seeking a pair already "broken."

And this carries me back to the time when we "did things" in the '60s.

Preparing a bunch of "long horns" just off the range for use in an outfit was a somewhat strenuous task; as apparently nothing kept them on the ground save their long horns.

In breaking them to the yoke we used to take them to the river bottom where the sand was deep, yoke them to a wagon with locked wheels, and then the circus began. Events happening in rapid succession during the introduction of this act that, to say the least, was exciting in the extreme, until the four-legged citizen from Texas either admitted defeat or broke his neck. No tree was too large for him to try to climb, no acrobatic feat too difficult to give it a whirl. The beautiful foliage overhanging and surrounding the arena might have curled up and dried from the overheated expressions from below, but in the end Mr. Bull admitted he had met his master for, in some manner, he was "broke."

It was often remarked that the "bull-whacker" was more generally addicted to the use of profane language than men in other occupations, but this I deny. I admit there were occasions when a manipulator of the wild bulls ran out of plain English and used words he hadn't been taught in the "primer class," but put any man in his place during a sudden Indian attack while on the road and he trying to work six yoke of "irresponsibles" into an improvised corral, at the same time trying to do a little execution with an old "muzzle-loader," the Indians all the time pouring in basketfulls of arrows into the outfit, making it appear like a traveling feather duster—if there is a man living who wouldn't say "turkey red" with the frills to it, why all I've got to say is that the individual has a right to claim his harp at once.

Like myself most of the bull-whackers had gone into the business young and had lost their opportunity for an education. Most of the bringing up, as was an old saying, came from our association with young fellows from the east, and young men from European countries who were second and third in a family of the aristocracy there. All were well educated, but the law of entail prevented them from having more than an allowance. These from love of excitement and the rapid going through of the last remittance from home, took this chance to see life as it was in the "wild and wooly West" at that time.

My first experience in bull-whacking was in 1864, the year generally conceded to be the worst for bad Indians. As far back as I can remember any of the red brothers I've had the misfortune to mix with were bad, and the closer the aquaintance the tougher he proved to be. Any of them would plunk you in the back while you were turned about to pour them a tin of coffee if the opportunity was favorable. I am reminded of "Shot-Mouth Charlie," as we used to call him, who was freighting with one of his own teams from Caddo Station, Indian Territory, to Fort Sill, Indian Territory, in the early '70s. He had climbed up on his wagon tongue to get more flour to make biscuits to serve two hungry buck visitors who had dropped in on him. Hearing a suspicious noise back of him he turned about in time to receive the contents of one of their guns across his face.

We have seen the aborigine from the Brazos, in Texas to Wyoming, but we never saw one I wanted to take home and raise as a pet. I would rather have a rattlesnake with seventeen rattles and an over-coat button for a tail piece. But I'm not hankering after either one.

As I was saying, my first experience in "whacking" was in 1864 when I was sent out with a number of others from Leavenworth, Kansas, to Diamond Springs, just west of Council Grove, Kansas, by the Stewart Stemens Co. of that city. The company had sent a train out and the men had corralled it at the Springs, the most of them refusing to go any further West, owing to the Indian scare out among the sagebrush. I had lately arrived West from my home in Michigan, in which state and the states of Indiana and Illinois, I had been trying to enlist in the army, but on account of my youth, height, and having no permit from my people, I had been turned down, and had come to the boundless West as a panacea for my disappointment.

The company was busy recruiting a bunch of bull-whackers to take the place of the "buckers" at the Springs, and I was accepted; the company, no doubt, considering under the circumstances, a "half loaf better than none." Thus it happened that on an early June day in 1864 there were dumped from a westbound coach at Diamond Springs, Kansas, as odd a collection of the human family as ever escaped the museums. The appearance of the bunch would have tempted the ancient mariner to cut loose from the bank and scuttle his ark had they come aboard during his high water experience. Generally speaking they were long on everything but money, clothes and religion.

Soon after our arrival in camp we tenderfeet were being instructed in the art of how to handle a wagon with a live end to it, and the proper manner of carrying an ox yoke and bow in yoking the cattle in preparation for hitching them to the wagons, being instructed by the wagon master and his assistant. A whip was given each driver of the outfit, the lash being about sixteen feet in length with a "popper" (whip cracker) added and fastened to a whip stock eighteen inches in length by a buckskin thong. This instrument of torture required an almost constant everyday manipulation by me during my first two hundred miles of the trip before I became proficient enough in handling it to prevent its going about my neck and hanging me. A gun was issued each man for protection of his life and property. Mine was just one remove from the blunderbuss vintage. Its Christian or baptismal name was the "Mississippi Yawger." Among its interesting adjuncts was a tape cap arrangement on the side of the lock, the original intention of its maker had been that in cocking the gun the side arrangement pushed the tape over the nipple of the piece, and the hammer striking the tape on the nipple ignited the priming below, thus saving the time of capping the gun in the old way. But a strong wind would often crowd the tape out of place. At times the tape became damp causing a misfire, and often at a very critical time. As a "has-previously-been" relic it could set up among the most ancient; but for actual every-day business it was a failure; though when it did try to make a record for itself, everything fore and aft recollected the effort made to be noticed.

Everything necessary for the handling of the train was furnished by the company, even to gunny sacks, for the buffalo chip depository.

We all carried ten-gallon kegs on the reach-poles of our wagons at the rear for water in case of long drives between drinks or of an accident on the road. Each man belonged to a particular mess, where he was supposed to have a vested right to seat himself on mother earth and fill up. All of my mess, except myself, were from Jackson, Clay and Platt counties, Mizzoo. All members of an overland freighter in the early days were called fictitious names foreign to his regular one. They dubbed me "Yank" and Yank I was during that trip. But a finer bunch to "stick," under any circumstances than our mess I've never seen.

An outfit was usually composed of twenty-six wagons—one mess, the other twenty-five freight, with six yoke of cattle to the wagon (12 cattle in all). There was with every outfit a bunch of loose cattle driven in the rear of the train by two extras. The loose cattle were called the "cavey yard" and were for use in case of an accident to the teams. The choir of such an outfit consisted of one wagon master and his assistant and two extras. These four rode mules. One night herder, who was supposed to sleep in the wagons while the train was on the move. If he did, I don't know how he managed to do so, for when one of those wagons fell into a rut it fell in with a chunk. And there were twenty-six irresponsible bull-whackers who walked and took the dust.

The bull-whackers received forty-five per and feed. Only a stomach capable of digesting feathers in a wad could long survive the stuff before indigestion took a fall out of it. Taos Lightning, or the "Mule Skinners' Delight" was frequently used as an antidote.[4] In the plains country the men and animals were frequently compelled to depend on buffalo wallows and soft mud deposits for water to supply their needs. In making camp the driver's first duty was to unyoke his cattle. After being unyoked, the cattle would invariably make directly for these water holes, riling up the already disagreeable appearing fluid and then stand in it to cool off, thus making it still more unpalatable for domestic use.

The greatest cost of framing up an outfit was the wagons and their furnishings. The steers in those days could be procurred by anyone going into the Southwest, rounding up a bunch of longhorns, and coming home with them with nothing to bother their conscience unless it might be an Indian arrow barb. Occasionally there would be a good singer in the crowd which, around the camp fire, was a treat. The songs were mostly war songs with "Brother Ike," "Days of Forty-nine," etc. Some Missourian once in awhile would break out like this:

"Oftimes I've wondered why women love men,
But more times I've wondered how men can love them."

Something like that tossed out over the prairie after night fall, waking up the timid wild animals, has, no doubt, been the cause of the Indians attacking us the next day.

There was always a few good story tellers in the outfit, of which I may give one or two poor imitations at some future time.

A few mornings after our coming to camp at the Springs the wagon master considering we "new uns" had learned sufficient to keep ourselves from under the moving wagon wheels, and after all had had an early breakfast, ordered the cattle turned into the wagon corral in preparation for the tenderfeet's first drive toward our destination, Fort Union, New Mexico. My previous experience in the bovine line having been with nothing more fierce than a milk

[4] Taos Lightning, a favorite liquor of the mountain men, was distilled at Taos, New Mexico.

cow, caused me to show up rather awkward in yoking any cattle into teams for my wagon. Consequently I got for mine the most unruly and meanest of the herd. Two of my teams were never unyoked during the whole trip. They were so contrary, though yoked together, they mutually agreed to disagree and always tried to pull in opposite directions. After the teams were hooked up to the wagons and everything being in shipshape to the captain's satisfaction, the big overland freighters (often called "prairie schooners") commenced to slowly drift toward the setting sun.

Part 2

I have given a description of breaking cattle to the yoke in the early '60s and of my being employed, amongst others, by the Stewart Stemens Company to pilot a wagon train loaded with government freight from Fort Leavenworth, Kansas, over the old Santa Fe trail to Fort Union, New Mexico.

It was early in the summer of 1864 when our outfit left Fort Leavenworth.

At that time there were but two places of habitation between Diamond Springs, west of Council Grove, Kansas, and Fort Lyons, Colorado, viz: Fort Larned, Kansas, and Bent's Fort, Colorado. At streams like Cow Creek, Turkey Creek, Jarvis Creek, Walnut Creek and ever at the Big Bend where there had been stage stations and stock ranches, all had been destroyed by our festive red brother.

The overland coaches we met, or that passed us, carried a military excort from Lyons going eastward, or Larned going west, to protect them from roving bands of Indians. The coaches could change horses on the route only at the two stations before named and the passengers were obliged to camp out on the road the same as the freighters. We met but three or four of these coaches on the entire trip and a "bull outfit" travels slow.

In western Kansas and eastern Colorado we traveled in two wings or columns. When on the road the wagonmaster rode some distance ahead of his train and at a signal from him or a warning from any direction the lead team of each column halted and the rear wheels of their wagons were immediately locked. Each succeeding rear wagon moved up in close order, the driver placing the fore wheel of his wagon snug against the rear inside wheel of the wagon in front of him in such a manner as to throw his cattle inside the wagon corral and locking his wheels, if occasion required it, thus forming a protection impregnable against the small arms carried by the Indians in those days.

The almost military system of handling a big freighting outfit at that time and having at least a portion of the men who were accustomed to that kind of life and all its duties, was the reason they were rarely worsted in their fights with the Indians.

Any careless handling of the train would have been taken advantage of by the reds. The Indian scout, posted at an advantageous point, might be signaling your condition to a hundred red painted devils, hidden in a neighboring arroyo at any time.

One occasionally heard of a pioneer or an emigrant train being wiped out, and frequently the cause was due to their own ignorance and in being unprepared. Often they were encumbered with women and children who were a hindrance to them in an Indian mixup and their inexperience placed their lives in jeopardy. The sight of an outfit coming on the plains with a fish pole and a string to it to handle cattle with would nearly cause a thoroughbred "bull-whacker" to throw a fit.

In a "bull outfit" all men had to be Johnny-on-the-spot. They used to tell a story about an old Indian chief going to a post commander and asking for ammunition. The commander refused him, saying he didn't intend to furnish him and his tribe material to kill his soldiers with. The chief retorted that he didn't want it for that purpose, but to kill bull-whackers—that his squaws could take sticks and whip his soldiers. Of course every-one knows that's a yarn, for our soldiers have given a good account of themselves in all our western history.

Each wagon carried a ten-gallon keg hung in the rear on a coupling pole which was kept filled with water for such emergencies as being forced to corral at any time through accident or an Indian attack.

Having had trouble just before coming to Fort Larned, the post commander ordered the wagonmaster to hold his train there and wait for other trains having government supplies, to come up and join us. We were in duty bound to comply with the order. After the post commander was satisfied as to numbers he allowed us to proceed on our way.

Soon after leaving the fort we were as badly separated as we were before reaching it, each outfit believing itself capable of taking care of all comers.

In all the distance between Diamond Springs and the mountains going out, we saw only one buffalo, and he was an old "has been," being divorced from the herd, "broke" (like a lot of us old-timers), with the coyotes on the rise of ground about him waiting for the opportunity to "hamstring" him and make his ending as miserable as possible. It being in the months of June and July, the buffaloes at that time of the year were feeding further north.

At the big bend of the Arkansas river a few black-tail deer showed themselves, but as quickly disappeared from view. We frequently saw small bands of antelope and other small game, but for such a vast expanse of unsettled territory the game was limited.

We met on the road before we came to the old Santa Fe crossing (dry route) a large Mexican outfit going to the Missouri river, their wagons loaded with the produce of their ranches and country. Their cattle were quite small—about the size of our two-year-olds back in the States. They drove (the bull-whackers called it herding) large numbers of them to each wagon. There were a few women with them who lifted the cover of their wagon to take a peep at us while we were passing. It made a fellow think of home and civilization then. Their faces were covered with some whitish preparation to preserve their complexions; it resembled a death mask.[5]

At the crossing, and just previous to making camp, we had a stampede, caused by the night herder, who was riding in a wagon near the rear of the train, shaking his blankets. His team commenced running and excited the others before it slowed to a pace a novice would consider impossible for oxen to make.

A cattle stampede and a horse or mule run-away can only be likened to a race between a team composed of a cyclone and a Texas norther hitched together racing a gentle summer Zephyr.

The cattle never quit going until they piled themselves into such a heap they could get no farther. There were steers with broken legs,

[5] Native New Mexican women used a variety of substances as a cosmetic to protect their faces from the sun, including chalk, clay, white ashes, and wheat flour.

besides scattered freight and damaged wagons, and it took a good week's work mending our wagon breaks with rawhides and such other material as we had with us in the train, and replenishing our lost stock from the cavey yard before we were able to continue our journey. Two of the wagons were without any rear wheels, the axles being kept off the ground by poles reaching from the front axle under the rear ones to the ground, and in this manner they went through the balance of the plains country and over the mountains into Fort Union, New Mexico. The poles had to be frequently renewed and the wagons were lightened of a portion of their freight by adding it to the mess and other wagons.

As I stated in my first article I, being a novice, at the first yoking drew a pair of which were never unyoked while on the trip. However, they came through the trouble without a blemish and as "ornery" as ever and happy besides, reminding one of the ancient saying, "The devil looks after his own."

The next camp of any importance we came to was Bent's Fort, on the Arkansas. We saw quite a few Cheyenne Indians at the post trading their plunder for such stores as Bent had that they wanted. We followed the river up to Fort Lyons and crossed the stream near there, going to Trinidad by way of Gray's ranch, and up the Purgatoire into Trinidad. There I first saw the conveyance used by the elite of the country—a burro fitted out with panniers and a Mexican sitting astride. The pannier on one side contained chickens and other produce while in the pocket on the other side was a yellow-skinned infant. The people, their dress, farming implements and their ways at the time called to the mind of the young tenderfoot scenes in the Bible.

In going up the Raton Pass, above Trinidad, to get on the summit of the range, we met one of the Major-Russell-Waddell outfits coming down. The men of their trains were called "The Bible Backs" by other freighters from the fact that their employer presented each of them with a Bible or Testament on their leaving the home station for a trip.

The pass in those days was surely equal to the "rocky road to Dublin," and from the conversation of the "B.B.'s" and the language they were using toward their cattle, one would infer the men had lost the "Word" in the bottom of the wagon. An early-day preacher advised his flock to refrain from using profane language, saying at no time was it excusable, unless they were whacking bulls. On the summit of the range we came to Dick Wootton's gate.[6] We found a train ahead of us whose wagonmaster was disputing with Wootton about the tolls. They were using some very heated talk in expressing their compliments to each other. The finish of it was, your Uncle Dick went in the house and came out with his "toll collector." I think the barrel of it was about as long as a fence rail— anyway, it got the money. Continuing, we journeyed on through by way of Maxwell's and thence to Fort Union, where we arrived without any unusual mishap, delivering our freight to the post quartermaster and ending a nine hundred and fifty mile trip in the old-fashioned rough-and-ready way.

The present-day traveler passing over the same route in the cars of the Santa Fe Rail-way can little imagine what it meant to make the trip over the trail when a settlement or even a water tank was lacking.

[6] On Uncle Dick Wootton's toll gate see note 12 of document 10, below.

10. Major John C. McFerran's Report and Journal, 1865

With the close of the Civil War in April, 1865, army troops in the
East became available for service along the Santa Fe Trail and other
western trails. During the previous four years, hostile Indians and
Confederate raiders had made travel to New Mexico a hazardous
undertaking. Indeed, during the Glorieta campaign in March of
1862, which culminated in the battle of Pigeon's Ranch, fifteen miles
east of Santa Fe, the far end of the trail had been virtually closed to
normal commercial traffic.

As part of the broad-range look that Washington officials were
taking at the needs of travelers to the southwestern territories, Q.M.
Gen. Montgomery C. Meigs ordered Maj. John Courts McFerran,
chief quartermaster of the military Department of New Mexico, to
prepare a report outlining the status of forts and describing the main
and alternate routes on the Santa Fe Trail, as they existed in the
summer of 1865.

Major McFerran, as a career army man, had a solid if
undistinguished record of service. A native of Kentucky, he had
graduated from West Point in 1843. He was stationed in south Texas
in May of 1846 and participated in the battles of Palo Alto and
Resaca de la Palma, which signaled the outbreak of the Mexican
War. In 1850 he was appointed chief commissary of the Department
of New Mexico, and during the ensuing decade he pulled quartermaster duty at various places in the territory, including Santa Fe and
Fort Union. In October, 1862, some six months after the last
Confederate forces had withdrawn to Texas, he was appointed chief
quartermaster of the department.[1]

---

[1] Biographical data for McFerran were drawn from George W. Cullum,
Biographical Register of the Officers and Graduates of the U.S. Military Academy, 2

When Major McFerran took charge of the quartermaster's books, they showed an accumulated indebtedness of $525,000, a figure attributable to the losses of supplies sustained during the recent Confederate invasion. The size of the debt had undermined governmental credit with private merchants and suppliers, and military certified vouchers were selling at a ruinous discount. McFerran claimed that by the summer of 1865, through the greatest of exertions, his department had managed to liquidate most of the outstanding debt, restore credit, and furnish the troops with the equipment they required. That had been achieved in spite of a series of natural disasters—insect plagues and drought followed by floods—that destroyed much of New Mexico's grain crop for a three-year period, necessitating the importation of high-priced corn from Fort Leavenworth.

In a letter to his superior, General Meigs, the major explained all of this and also took note of the way in which military freighting was handled on the Santa Fe Trail: "The sources of supplies for troops in the department [are] St. Louis, Missouri, Fort Leavenworth, Kansas, and other points east of those. From Fort Leavenworth the transportation of these supplies is by ox and mule wagons, through the Indian country, a distance of seven hundred and fifty miles to the main depot of the department at Fort Union, New Mexico.[2] Then they are received and stored, and from thence distributed as required, by wagon transportation, to the various posts and commands. Their distribution as well as transportation from Fort Leavenworth to the depot, Fort Union, is done by contract, awarded to the lowest responsible bidder, after due public notice; that from Fort Leavenworth to Fort Union being given out by the depot quartermaster at Fort Leavenworth, and that from Fort Union to the various posts by the chief quartermaster, department of New Mexico. This course I consider the best for the United States."[3]

vols. (New York: D. Van Nostrand, 1868), 2:96; and Francis B. Heitman, *Historical Register and Dictionary of the United States Army*, 2 vols. (Washington, D.C.: Government Printing Office, 1903), 1:665.

[2] Fort Union was founded in 1851, about twenty-four miles northeast of Las Vegas, near the junction of the Mountain Branch and the Cimarron Cut-off. It functioned as a quartermaster depot, and its troops, in concert with those from Forts Larned and Dodge, patroled the western half of the Santa Fe Trail.

[3] McFerran to Meigs, Washington, D.C., July 26, 1865, in United States, 39th Cong., 1st sess., *House Executive Documents*, no. 1 (ser. 1249), Report of the Secretary of War, vol. 1 (Washington, D.C., 1865), p. 750.

Major McFerran himself seems to have made numerous trips over the Santa Fe Trail in the line of duty. It is known, for example, that he was in charge of a detachment that drove cavalry horses and conveyed governmental funds to New Mexico in 1860.[4] Another journey of record took place in the summer of 1864, when he traveled between Kansas City and Santa Fe while Indian disturbances in Kansas were at their peak. On that occasion, he wrote: "Both life and property on this route is almost at the mercy of the Indians. Every tribe that frequents the plains is engaged in daily depredations on trains, and immense losses to the Government and individuals have occurred, and many lives have already been lost."[5]

In his report and journal for 1865, which appear below, McFerran provides useful data with regard to military supply and transportation on the Santa Fe Trail.[6] His renderings of place names of Spanish, French, or Indian origin are badly mangled; therefore I have supplied accepted spellings in brackets.

The Report

Washington, D.C., July 27, 1865.

General: At your request, I furnish you with the following data, obtained in my recent trip from Santa Fé, New Mexico, to Fort Leavenworth, Kansas.

There are two old and well-established routes from Fort Union (the main depot of supplies for the troops in New Mexico) to Fort Leavenworth, viz: the "Raton" and the "Cimarron" routes. The former passes over the Raton mountain, crossing the Pingatorie [Purgatoire] and Timpia [Timpas] rivers and the Arkansas river at Bent's Old Fort; then down that stream, passing Fort Lyon, Colorado Territory, forty miles below; thence ninety miles to Choteau's [Chouteau's] island, where it unites with a branch of the Cimarron route, called Aubrey's [Aubry's] Cut-off; thence down the river eighty miles to where the Cimarron route crosses the Arkansas

[4] Cullum, *Biographical Register,* 2:96.

[5] Oliva, *Soldiers on the Santa Fe Trail,* pp. 155–56.

[6] The report and journal are incorporated in the Report of the Secretary of War for 1865, cited in note 3 above.

river. The two routes unite at this point, known as the Cimarron crossing, and form one route to Fort Leavenworth. The grass on the Raton route is generally good and abundant, but the distance is one hundred miles further than by the Cimarron, and the road is much worse. Fort Lyon, on the Raton route, is a collection of stone buildings erected in 1860–'61 by six companies of the then first United States cavalry, under the late General [John] Sedgwick, then lieutenant colonel of that regiment.[7] Nothing of any consequence has been done to the buildings since he left them. They are incomplete, but habitable, and are, or were as I passed, occupied, I believe, by three small companies of Colorado volunteers. The animals, both horses and mules, of this command, were not in very good order, which was attributed to the want of grain, of which they had been without entirely for several months until a few days before I passed, when a large supply was received from Fort Leavenworth. The grain for this post should come from the settlements on the Arkansas river, which commence some sixty-five miles above the post, and from those on the Hunfans [Huerfano] and Pingatorie [Purgatoire] rivers, tributaries of the Arkansas from the south, and from which it could be hauled at certainly less expense than from Fort Leavenworth. The crops through the section above referred to I examined closely, and they promise an abundant harvest. Hay can be had in any quantity within from three to ten miles of the post, and should not cost over fifteen or twenty dollars per ton, delivered and stacked. The quartermaster and commissary stores are in some buildings known as Bent's New Fort, about one mile below, on the river. It would, I think, be better if the post were completed and the stores provided with storage there.

The Cimarron route branches off from the Raton at or near Fort Union in a northeasterly direction, crosses the Ocato [Ocaté] creek, Red [Canadian] river, McHus [McNees], Whetstone, and Rabbit Ear creeks, Cimarron river where the Aubrey [Aubry] Cut-off branches in a northern direction, Sand creek, and a sand desert of fifty or sixty miles, to the Arkansas river, which it crosses, uniting with the Raton route. The grass on the Cimarron route is as good as on the other, but the fuel and water not so plentiful; yet there is

[7] General Sedgewick died at the Civil War battle of Spottsylvania, Virginia, on May 9, 1864.

enough for passing trains. During very dry seasons the water is quite scarce, and some of it, especially at the Cimarron river, is brackish. It is the route, however, generally travelled by merchants' trains, and now that rebel raids from Arkansas and Texas are not to be feared, should be the route travelled by the government contractors, as it is nearly, if not quite, one hundred miles shorter than the Raton route, and the contract is so much per one hundred pounds per one hundred miles. The only encampment of troops on this route is at Cedar bluffs, a point near what is known as Upper Cimarron spring, about one hundred and forty miles from Fort Union, or nearly halfway between that post and the Cimarron crossing, which is just three hundred miles. This encampment consists of three companies of volunteers under Colonel Christopher Carson, and is supplied from Fort Union.[8] The command will return to Fort Union in November. A permanent camp or post should be established on this route at or near the present one of Colonel Carson's, where fuel and water can be procured in sufficient quantities. Three companies, one of cavalry and two of infantry, would suffice for the garrison.

From the Cimarron crossing, where the two routes unite, the road passes down the river about thirty miles to Fort Dodge. This post consists of a few huts made of poles set endwise in the ground and covered with dirt and tents, enclosed by a ditch and a dirt embankment, and garrisoned, I believe, by five companies of volunteers under a Major [William F.] Armstrong. A few days before I passed two Indians drove off almost all the public animals from this post. These had hardly gotten the stock away before a large number of their people, estimated variously at from 500 to 5,000, showed themselves on the surrounding hills.

The grain for Fort Dodge is hauled from Forts Riley and Leavenworth. Hay is abundant in the river bottom near the post, and should not cost over twenty dollars per ton, delivered and stacked. Fuel and building material, like that used in making the huts that they now have, can, I was informed by the post quartermaster, be obtained in sufficient quantities within fifteen miles of the post on either side of the river.

[8] The encampment at Cedar Bluffs was Camp (or Fort) Nichols, which was established on June 1, 1865, by Col. Kit Carson to protect the Santa Fe Trail. The site was in the Oklahoma Panhandle, about five miles east of the New Mexico boundary.

From Fort Lyon to Fort Dodge, a distance of about two hundred miles, there are no troops. I am of the opinion that a four-company post, two of cavalry and two of infantry, should be established about half way between these two posts, and that if the troops were active it would protect the travel more from the Indians than anything else that could be done.[9]

The road passes down the river from Fort Dodge for some eight or ten miles, there divides—one part, of one hundred miles in length, following the river, with plenty of water; the other passing over the ridge, without water in dry seasons, cutting off some thirty miles, and uniting with the river route at Fort Larned, on Pawnee fork. Fuel on these two roads is scarce, and trains are almost entirely dependent for it on the dried excrement of buffalo and the cattle of trains, familiarly known as "buffalo chips." The grass is good.

Fort Larned is a post of four companies, some sixty-five miles by the ridge road and one hundred miles by the river road, below Fort Dodge. It was built in 1858, '59, and '60, of logs set endwise in the ground and roofed with earth. It is on the Pawnee fork, but too far from the road, is surrounded by an abundance of fuel, water, and good grazing. Hay can be cut within a few miles of the post, at a cost, I should think, of about twenty dollars per ton, delivered. It is a proper place for a military post, and should be the depot of supplies for any troops acting against Indians on that line. The grain for this post comes from Forts Riley and Leavenworth. It can and should come from the country around Council Grove and Fort Riley, and thus save at least transporting it one hundred miles.

At Fort Larned the road again divides, one part, a new route, by way of Fort Riley, Kansas. There are troops on this route at Fort Ellsworth, where the road crosses the Smoky Hill fork of the Kansas river, at Fort Riley and at Topeka. The other route (the old Santa Fé trail) continues down the Arkansas river some fifty miles, crosses Walnut, Cow, and Little Arkansas creeks, to Council Grove, at all of which points are troops; thence via Burlingame and Lawrence, to Fort Leavenworth, Kansas.

For any further information with regard to distance, &c., I

[9] To meet this need the new post of Fort Aubry was placed in the following September, 1865, astride the trail in present Hamilton County, Kansas, three miles east of the town of Syracuse.

would respectfully refer you to the accompanying journal of my last trip across the plains.

Very respectfully, your obedient servant,

J. C. McFerran

Major and Quartermaster

Brevet Major General M. C. Meigs,

Quartermaster General U.S.A., Washington, D.C.

The Journal

Washington, D.C., October 4, 1865

General: In obedience to verbal orders from you, I submit the following as my report of my recent trip from Santa Fé, New Mexico, to Fort Leavenworth, Kansas:

I left Santa Fé June 5, 1865; traveled twenty-five miles through pine and piñon timber, with fine water and grass, and over a fair road to Kosloski's [Kozlowski's] ranche.[10]

June 6.—Left Kosloski's at 6 a.m.; passed over the same character of country, twenty-two miles, to the town of San José; there crossed the Pecos river, a beautiful mountain stream; continued on ten miles to Bemal [Bernal] spring, and camped, with wood, water, and good grass; road good, as a general thing; traveled thirty-two miles.

June 7.—Left camp at 6½ a.m.; marched five miles over a bad road, well timbered and good grass, to the town of Iscolate [Tecolote], on a creek of the same name; twelve miles further over a good road through a wooded country to Los [Las] Vegas, on the Rio Gallenos [Gallinas]. From this place two roads lead to Fort Union, called respectively "the long" and "the short" routes, the former being five miles longer than the latter; I traveled over the long route, a smooth prairie, and generally used, to the Rio Sapio [Sapello], seventeen miles; crossed that stream and camped, having traveled that day thirty-four miles.

[10] Martin Kozlowski's ranch and stage station were located on the Santa Fe Trail, one-half mile southeast of the Pecos Pueblo ruins.

June 8.—Left camp at 6½ a.m.; marched one and a half mile, and crossed the Rio Moro [Mora] at Watson's and Kroimg's [Kronig's] ranche; then six miles further, and camped at Fort Union, lying over the rest of the day for a refit, escort, rations, &c.

June 9.—Left camp at 7½ a.m., travelling by the "Raton" route over a rolling prairie eighteen miles to the Rio Ocaté, one of the points from which hay is procured for Fort Union; continued twelve miles further to Sweet Water creek and camped; wood, water, and grass abundant; road bad; distance travelled, thirty miles.

June 10.—Left camp, passing over a wretchedly bad road for ten miles through the town of Rayado, crossing a stream of same name at the town; marched over a rough, broken, and hilly road twelve miles further to Maxwell's ranche, where crossed the Colorado Chiquito [Cimarron] river;[11] two miles further crossed the Rio Ponio [Poñil], and camped on the hills one mile this side, making twenty-three miles this day. Road very bad, but wood, water and grass in plenty.

June 11.—Left camp at 6½ a.m.; marched fourteen miles over a good road to Rio Vennejo [Vermejo]; bad crossing; twenty-three miles further brought me to the Red [Canadian] river, where camped; wood, water, and grass good. Marched thirty-seven miles.

June 12.—Left camp at 6½ a.m.; crossed Red [Canadian] river; marched ten miles, and commenced the ascent of the Raton mountains, four miles to the summit; descended three miles, struck a mountain stream and a good road, with a toll-gate on it,[12] thirteen

[11] The headquarters of Lucien B. Maxwell's huge ranch faced the plaza at the village of Cimarron. The owner maintained an open door, freely feeding and housing travelers on the Santa Fe Trail.

The Colorado Chiquito, or Little Colorado River, is now called the Cimarron. It flows through the village of Cimarron and later joins the Canadian (formerly called the Colorado, or Red River) four miles from Springer, New Mexico. This small Cimarron is distinct from the larger, better-known Cimarron, a tributary of the Arkansas that flows through the Oklahoma Panhandle and southwestern Kansas.

[12] The accepted date for the opening of Uncle Dick Wootton's toll gate in Raton Pass is 1866. McFerran's statement, however, indicates that the gate was in operation as early as June, 1865, while document 9 above, by Vanderwalker, suggests that it was open in 1864.

miles further to the town of Trinidad, Colorado Territory, on the Rio Pingatoire [Purgatoire]; crossed the stream, and passing on one mile, camped with wood, water, and grass plenty; marched thirty-one miles. Hearing that the Arkansas river was not fordable at Bent's Old Fort, the usual crossing of the Raton route, I concluded to strike directly north for a bridge near Pueblo, Colorado Territory, where I could certainly cross the river, although it was fully one hundred and forty miles out of my way.

June 13.—Left camp at 6 a.m.; moved over rolling prairie road, with fine grass and timber in spots, but no water; thirty-five miles to water-holes, and camped.

June 14.—Left camp at 6 a.m.; passed over same class of country twenty-five miles to the Rio Huressamo [Huerfano], at Craig's ranche, and camped with wood, water, and grass abundant.

June 15—Left camp at 1 p.m.; marched twelve miles; crossed the Greenhorn creek, and camped; wood, water, and grass plenty.

June 16.—Left camp at 6 a.m.; marched four miles; crossed the Rio San Carlos; marched nine miles, and crossed the Arkansas river on a common bridge, made of poles or logs laid from bank to bank, with a rude pole flooring. The river banks at this place are of solid rock, fifteen feet above high water, and the river itself is not over thirty-five feet wide, if that. From here struck down the Arkansas; marched seven miles to the town of Pueblo; two miles further passed the Fontaine que Bouche [Fontaine Que Bouille, or Boiling Fountain Creek], a tributary from the north to the Arkansas; traveled ten miles further, passing fine farms, and camped with wood, water, and grass.

June 17.—Left camp at 6 a.m., travelling down the river forty miles, over a good road, passing many farms, and camped with wood, water, and grass.

June 18.—Left camp at 6 a.m.; marched twenty-eight miles down the Arkansas to Bent's Old Fort; continued on fourteen miles, and camped with good grass and water; wood scarce; made forty-two miles.

June 19.—Started at 6 a.m.; marched twenty-six miles down the river to Fort Lyon; camped for four hours to draw rations, shoe animals, and refit; at 3 p.m. started; marched twelve miles and camped on the river for the night.

June 20.—Left camp at 6 a.m.; continued down the Arkansas thirty-five miles, and camped; road good, grass plenty, and wood in clumps of cottonwood along the river.

June 21.—Left camp at 6 a.m.; marched thirty-six miles to camp, following the course of the river, sometimes close to its bank, and at others passing over spurs of hills one, two, and three miles from the river; grass and water abundant, with buffalo chips for fuel.

June 22.—Left camp at 5½ a.m.; marched five miles to Choteau's [Chouteau's] island, where Aubrey's [Aubry's] Cut-off crosses the river and joins the Raton route; marched forty miles and camped on the river; road good; grass and water good; fuel scarce, being buffalo chips.

June 23.—Left camp at 6 a.m.; marched twenty-eight miles to Fort Dodge; thence fifteen miles to ponds of water on the ridge route, and camped.

June 24.—Left camp at 5 a.m.; marched forty-five miles, and camped near Fort Larned. From that point followed the old Santa Fé trail to Fort Leavenworth, Kansas, where I arrived July 4, 1865, just thirty days from Santa Fé, having traveled about nine hundred miles.

All of which is respectfully submitted.

J. C. McFerran,
Major and Quartermaster.

Brevet Major General M. C. Meigs,
Quartermaster General U.S.A., Washington, D.C.

11. Captain Charles Christy's Memoirs, 1867

Charles Christy was seventy-three years old and a resident of Denver in 1908 when he completed his memoirs, detailing an adventurous period of his early life, 1850 to 1880, during which he had been a hunter, fur trapper, and United States government scout. One section of those memoirs dealt with his experiences at Fort Zarah and Plum Buttes on the Santa Fe Trail in central Kansas.[1] Integral to this part of his story is the account of the massacre involving a part of the wagon train of Franz Huning, who is incorrectly called Frank Hunig by Christy.

As already recounted in the introduction to Ernestine Huning's diary, document 8, her husband, Franz, was a prominent Albuquerque trader who made frequent trips over the trail. During the spring of 1867 he started east with five wagons. In April he encountered the expedition of Maj. Gen. Winfield Scott Hancock, who was camped at Fort Larned. The soldiers were holding a council with the Cheyennes for the purpose of reminding the Indians of treaty obligations assumed in 1865 that required the tribe to remain south of the Arkansas River. The Indians soon slipped away, abandoning their camp; and one of Hancock's subordinates, Lt. Col. George A. Custer, went in pursuit. When Hancock learned that the fugitives had burned a stage station on the Smoky Hill route to the north, he destroyed the abandoned teepee village in reprisal.

---

[1] The portion of the memoirs that is reprinted here first appeared in *The Trail* 1 (Jan., 1909): 13-19, under the title "The Personal Memoirs of Capt. Chas. Christy," with an editorial note by Clarence Lower. I obtained a copy through the courtesy of the Colorado Historical Society, Denver. Fort Zarah was established on September 6, 1864, to guard the Santa Fe Trail. It was located on the east side of Walnut Creek, about three miles east of the present town of Great Bend.

As Franz Huning himself explained, these events bore directly on his own subsequent tragedy. Of the Hancock campaign, he wrote: "The whole big demonstration was a complete failure since it only served to make the Indians right good and mad by burning of their tents, equipments and utensils. Consequently they went on the warpath for about two years, causing a great deal of damage on settlements and the commerce on the plains. I myself later became a victim of their revenge."[2]

Arriving in St. Louis, Franz went on to Dayton, Ohio, to meet Ernestine's mother and her youngest son, Fritz, who were to accompany him back to New Mexico. From Dayton they proceeded to the new railhead at Junction City, Kansas, where Huning was to rendezvous with his caravan. From New Mexico he had brought five of his own freight wagons. To these were now added a barouche, a sort of fancy carriage with its driver, for the transportation of his in-laws as well as extra ammunition.[3] *Efforts to unite with a larger party, for safety reasons, proved futile because, as Franz observes, "other trains were too far behind to wait for or too far ahead to overtake. I therefore determined to travel alone as far as Fort Zarah or Larned, and wait there until a regular convoy should be organized, as prescribed by the "Military."*[4] *This proved to be a fatal gamble.*

From Junction City the little caravan, in early September, made its way southwestward, joining the main Santa Fe Trail at Lost Spring. Continuing on to the Little Arkansas crossing, Franz was surprised to find a company of soldiers temporarily stationed there. Unfortunately, the captain in charge turned down Franz's request for an escort, even though signs of hostile Indians were everywhere in evidence along the trail.

Soon after leaving the crossing, the small caravan was passed by two army wagons that belonged to the unit just visited. Complained Franz bitterly: "One of the wagons [was] full of negro wenches and the other one with an escort for said wenches besides some horsemen. They were bound on a pleasure excursion to a creek

[2] Browne, *Trader on the Santa Fe Trail*, p. 88.
[3] The barouche, a covered carriage, was available at that date in several styles and sizes (see G. & D. *Cook & Sons Illustrated Catalog of Carriages* [New Haven, Conn.: Baker & Goodwin Printers, 1860; reprint, New York: Dover Publications, 1970], pp. 195, 199).
[4] Browne, *Trader on the Santa Fe Trail*, p. 89.

about 10 or 12 miles away to hunt plums!! The Captain had plenty of men to spare to escort his wenches on a plum hunt, but to protect the lives and property of the travelers he had none."[5]

About three o'clock that afternoon, Huning and his company crossed Cow Creek in eastern Rice County and headed toward Plum Buttes. The buttes were really a collection of low sandhills, surrounded by dense plum thickets, lying midway between Cow Creek and the Great Bend of the Arkansas River. As the party approached these heights, howling warriors suddenly attacked the train. The assailants were predominantly Cheyennes, with a sprinkling of Kiowas and Arapahoes.

For details of what ensued, one can refer to several different, contradictory accounts, including that of Captain Christy, who reached the scene soon after the raid. Within the ensuing few days, Franz wrote several letters to Ernestine, telling about the deaths of her mother and brother. Long afterward, in his memoirs, he gave a full description of the sorrowful event, but by then his recollections varied considerably from what he had originally told his wife. Both the memoirs and the letters were published by Huning's granddaughter in 1973.[6]

His grandson Harvey Fergusson provides another abbreviated version in his own autobiography. In summarizing his grandfather's career, he tells of the Plum Buttes massacre. He may have obtained his information directly from Franz or Ernestine; or perhaps he got it secondhand from other family members. Strangely, he produces details that are not found in either Franz's letters or memoirs, and in fact he includes data that are at variance with those of his grandfather.[7]

The reminiscences of Great Bend pioneer Homer H. Kidder contain an interesting paragraph regarding the massacre: "During the fall of 1867 the Indians attacked a mule train, enroute for [New] Mexico, near the mouth of Walnut Creek, cut off an ambulance from the rear end and killed an old lady and gentleman, cut the old lady in quarters, piled her clothes on the remains and set them on fire, and carried off the bleeding scalps of both at their belts."[8]

---

[5] Ibid.
[6] Ibid., pp. 88–96.
[7] Fergusson, *Home in the West*, pp. 38–40.
[8] *Biographical History of Barton County, Kansas*, p. 16.

Note that Kidder says Huning's in-laws were riding in an ambulance (a popular conveyance for civilian travelers), as does Harvey Fergusson. But Franz, as indicated, declared that they were occupying a barouche, while Christy says they were riding in a covered wagon. Again, by Kidder's account, the doomed lady and her son (the gentleman) were lagging at the rear, while Franz claims they were amidst the wagons, and Christy reports that they had been riding far ahead of the train, with Franz out front on mule back.

By his own testimony, as set down in his memoirs, Franz Huning was in a state of shock both during and immediately after the massacre. "I had been so bewildered," he avows, "that I didn't think that I knew what I was doing." Farther on he adds: "Some of the incidents of the attacks at Plum Buttes I did not remember till months afterwards, they were crowded into a few moments like a flash."9 That condition of mind could explain the conflicting statements that he made on later occasions. There might, however, be more to it than that.

According to Franz's version of the attack, he managed to circle the wagons and mount a defense. The vehicle bearing his relatives had run into the Indian lines at the first assault, and he gave brief thought to going in pursuit. But he explains that a moment's reflection convinced him that it would be madness, since he and his men had only a half-dozen shots left for their guns. Later he made a daring ride to Fort Zarah for help and returned with the relief party.

Captain Christy's rendering of the story diverges at numerous points. Most significantly he maintains that "the moment the Indians appeared Huning clapped spurs to his horse and took to flight leaving the others of his party to make their escape as best they could." Rather than seeing this as an act of cowardice, the captain expresses the belief that had Franz stayed to fight, he would have "met a horrible death and he did wisely to escape while he could."

If we give greater weight to the testimony of the scout than to that of the trader, it would appear that, in fact, Franz Huning did succumb to panic, a circumstance that could well account for his professed confusion and lapse of memory. Captain Christy, however, also erred in a number of particulars (as indicated in the editorial notes) when it came time years later to compose his memoirs, so that

9 Browne, *Trader on the Santa Fe Trail*, pp. 92, 94.

it is seemingly impossible at this date to sort out all of these discrepancies satisfactorily.

Contradictions aside, there is no question that Franz Huning sustained the loss of his mother-in-law and her son, along with their driver. Largely because records of the incident have not been readily accessible, the Plum Buttes massacre has failed to find a place in the general histories of the Santa Fe Trail. With the publication of the Huning account (in 1973) and with the republication here of Captain Christy's long-buried memoir, that deficiency can easily be remedied.

One final bit of information relevant to this story is that farmers who later settled along the trail just east of Plum Buttes often plowed up charred remains of one or more wagons, as well as domestic items, which led to the popular belief that a Santa Fe caravan had here met destruction at the hands of Indians. In 1876 the Rice County Gazette *reported that on his section, resident William McGee had found "broken and partly burned wagons, plows, barrels, tubs, boxes and earthenware; and for miles around lay scattered unworn boots and shoes, crisped by prairie fires and the scorching sun, with other articles—everything denoting the place to have been the scene of a general massacre."* [10]

The current owner of this battleground, Ralph Hathaway of Chase, Kansas, has carefully preserved a one-half-mile stretch of deeply scored wheel ruts of the Santa Fe Trail. He says: "When my grandparents, John L. and Mary E. Hathaway, arrived here from Lee County, Iowa in 1878, they discovered signs of the massacre. While breaking sod along the east side of his homestead John L. and his sons turned up several articles—a pistol, a watch, and many pieces of hardware from burned wagons. . . . The only artifacts we have found [today] were broken bits of ironstone china and a few large caliber bullets." [11]

Since the route from Cow Creek to Plum Buttes and westward to Pawnee Rock was one of the most dangerous segments of the Santa Fe Trail, particularly during the severe Indian troubles of the 1860s, it is quite possible that more than one caravan was lost in the vicinity

[10] John M. Muscott, "The History of Rice County," in the *Rice County Gazette* (Sterling, Kans.), Mar. 30, 1876; a separate reprint was issued by Max Moxley of Sterling in 1976.

[11] Ralph Hathaway, *My One-half Mile of Santa Fe Trail* (Ellsworth, Kans.: Ellsworth Printing Co., 1984), p. 6.

of Hathaway's farm. Notwithstanding, it is plausible to assume that many of the blackened relics collected over the past century east of the Buttes are actually the grim evidence of Franz Huning's personal tragedy on that bitter September day in 1867.

Expressing sympathy for the Indian is to my mind worse than the habit women have of sending flowers to a wife-murderer. There has been a noticeable tendency among some story writers, and among those of the Fenimore Cooper kind in particular, to throw a hero's halo around the Indian. I am very much opposed to this. I have been among the Indians nearly all my life, and have seen them under all conditions, but I cannot say that I can recall any one of the whole lot who, by any stretch of the imagination, could be called a hero or anything approaching it. All the old scouts and Indian fighters will say the same, and the statement is true. Nowadays an Indian is seldom seen outside of a Wild West show, and the younger generations gather their ideas of him mainly from dime novels and other works of fiction. I am satisfied that Cooper's Indian tales, written so many years ago, have indirectly caused the deaths of hundreds of whites and reds. The stories invested the Indian with many excellent qualities which he did not possess, and created a sentiment for him which was unmerited and which protected him when deserving punishment. Elated at escaping so frequently the penalty of his misdeeds the noble red man felt encouraged to repeat and increase his outrages, until finally it became necessary to kill off a lot of them; and I am pleased to say that it has fallen to my fortune to have taken a prominent part in bringing about this last good work, of making "good" Indians out of bad ones. Let me relate a few more of my experiences with the redskins, incidents which have occurred under my own observation, and adventures in which I have taken an active part. I wish that the simple facts of the horrible outrages and mutilations that I have seen might be told in plain words so that all could understand, for then the reader would get a true view of the Fenimore Cooper Indian.

Back in 1866 I was government scout at Fort Zarrah, on the Arkansas River, at the mouth of Walnut Creek. Fort Zarrah was not a formidable fortification. It had only a few soldiers in its garrison. It was more of a stage station than a fort, and rarely more than fifteen or twenty soldiers were detailed there at a time. The soldiers acted as escorts to stage-coaches and freight-wagons, to protect them from the attacks of hostile Indians, and they came and went every day. The war of the confederated tribes against the government had dragged along for two years; but the close of the Civil War relieved the government of the drain upon its troops and it was now able to throw the full strength of its army into the field against the Indians. Fights and skirmishes were of daily occurrence. The Indians constantly watched their opportunity, lying in wait to cut off any stray party of whites that happened to come their way—whether troops or settlers made no difference.

One day a man by the name of Frank Hunig rode into Fort Zarrah with the startling announcement that a band of two hundred Cheyennes had surprised his party at Plum Buttes, seven miles below on the Arkansas, and by that time had probably massacred them all. Hunig had made his escape and had come to the fort for assistance. There was little we could do in that direction, as there were only a few soldiers at the fort, and we had no horses—when we went as escorts we rode from station to station on the coaches. Nevertheless, as soon as Hunig made known his news, the soldiers hustled as fast as they could. Since there was no other way to get to the scene of the massacre they fell in line and started to march. They were well armed and eager for a fight, but they had little hope of meeting the Indians by the time they arrived, nor of finding any of the victims alive.

As I was scout of the fort the commandant ordered me to get to the scene as quickly as possible. I harnessed four of the fastest mules to an ambulance, and taking with me for my fighting partner a little Mexican named Roma, we started for the Buttes on a keen jump.[12] We left the soldiers to follow after us on foot as best they might and were soon out of sight.

Hunig followed with the soldiers. He was a freighter and had been on his way over the Santa Fe trail with a bull-train bound for Albuquerque, New Mexico. Accompanied by his wife, his sister and his brother-in-law, he had driven some miles ahead of the bull-train in a covered wagon, not thinking of danger, when they were

---

[12] Since Roma is neither a standard first or last name in Spanish, it is possible that Christy's memory failed and it should have been Romero, a common surname in New Mexico.

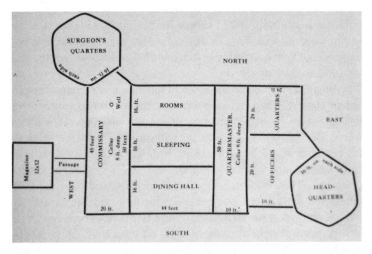

Plan of Fort Zarah (after Bernard Bryan Smyth, The Heart of the New Kansas *[Great Bend, Kans.: B. B. Smyth, Book and Job Printer, 1880]).*

---

suddenly cut off by a war party of Indians who charged furiously upon them from over the brow of a knoll.[13] The moment the Indians appeared Hunig clapped spurs to his horse and took to flight leaving the others of his party to make their escape as best they could. Hunig had been fortunate enough to give the Indians the slip, and knowing Fort Zarrah to be the nearest military post he had made the best of his way there for aid. Had he stayed with his party to fight the Indians he would have met a horrible death and he did wisely to escape while he could.

Roma and I drove to the scene of the massacre as fast as our mules could take us. The ambulance flew along, hitting only the high places. I kept the lash singing on the mules and we made a scorching race. Roma and I were armed to the teeth and spoiling for a fight. We had no fear of any number of red devils we might run into—the more the better.

Roma was a little Mexican but he was one of the bravest fighters I ever saw. He had no fear of anything living, and fighting Indians was as the breath in his nostrils. When about to go into a

[13] Christy is clearly mistaken when he states that Franz was accompanied by his wife and sister.

fight, he would strip naked except for his cartridge belt. Then he would wade into the reds wildeyed; and a troop from the infernal regions could not have stopped Roma until the fight was finished and the Indians were on the run.

When we arrived on the scene of the massacre there was not an Indian in sight. They were too wise to remain. They knew one man had gotten away in the direction of the fort and that the soldiers would soon be coming. Besides the bull-train was but a few miles in the rear and would be approaching with its company of freighters and the Indians wanted no fight with soldiers and freighters combined. Therefore, as soon as they had finished their work of killing the party and looting the wagon, they had beaten a hasty retreat, and when we arrived they were nowhere to be seen.

A dreadful sight met our eyes. On all sides were the evidences of a terrific struggle. Everything that had been in the wagon was strewn on the ground and stained with blood. The wagon had been burned and what remained of it was riddled with bullets; even the spokes of the wheels had been cut to pieces. Lying under the wagon we found the naked body of the man, scalped and hacked in a horrible manner. That he had fought desperately ere going down was evident; but if he had killed any of them the Indians had carried away the bodies, as none were lying around. Hidden among the feathers in the ticking of a feather-bed we found the bodies of the two women, both naked and disembowelled and with their breasts cut off.[14]

Roma and I gathered up the three bodies and placed them in the bottom of the ambulance. Then we drove back toward the fort. Our mules were tired by their rapid run and we jogged slowly along, keeping a lookout meanwhile for the bull-train which Hunig had said should be somewhere in the vicinity, but we could see nothing of it.

When we were scarcely a mile on our return there came suddenly streaming from a distant copse on our right a body of mounted Indians who rode galloping towards us, firing and yelling as they came. I knew what was cut out for us then and I began throwing the lash into the mules. After killing the party, the Indians had withdrawn only a little way and had secreted themselves in a

[14] The man found under the wagon must have been the driver. The mutilated condition of the two bodies inside may have led the narrator to conclude that they were both women, when in fact they were Franz's mother-in-law and her young son, Fritz.

copse to await developments. When only one ambulance drove up and they watched Roma and me gather up the bodies, the redskins thought we were the only ones who had been sent out from the fort for that purpose, and when we drove away they decided to catch us and kill us, too; and so they rode out from their concealment and came after us in hot chase. When the Indians came yelling into view I gave no more thought to our mules as to whether they were rested, but sent the lash whistling around their legs and they sprang forward and we bent bounding along the trail again at another mile-a-minute speed.

The Indians let out a war-whoop that warned us what we were to expect and came after us at redoubled speed. Their ponies stretched forward in a sweeping gallop and bullets and arrows began to sing about our ears. It would have been certain death for us to stop to fight, for the Indians hopelessly outnumbered us. It became now a race for life and our one hope was to keep ahead until they saw the soldiers coming, when I knew the cowardly redskins would leave us and run away, even though they might outnumber us twenty to one.

The little Mexican faced the rear and sat astride the bodies in the bottom of the ambulance; and as we raced along, bumping over hillocks and holes, Roma fired back at the Indians, keeping the bullets flying from his carbine as fast as he could. This checked the chase a little as the Indians halted every now and then to return his fire, and this gave us an opportunity to increase our distance. Their bullets struck the ambulance from time to time but Roma and I fortunately escaped being hit by any of them.

I could not help Roma with the shooting because it was my job to keep the mules moving. I was up in front on the driver's seat, handling the reins and encouraging the mules by voice and whip. As for the mules they were doing their part nobly; they leaned well in their collars and settled down to a pace that made their legs look like fringe, while they flew along like birds.

With the help of Roma's gun we held our distance in advance of the yelling horde for four miles, when by that time we saw the dust raised by the soldiers, who were approaching in the distance on the double-quick; then, with a parting yell and volley, the Indians turned and rode away and we saw them no more. The soldiers having come up with us Roma and I were safe and we resumed our way to the fort at a more leisurely pace. The bodies of the victims were buried near the fort and a few days later, when the bull-train arrived, Hunig rejoined it and continued his way to Albuquerque.[15]

The massacre of the Hunigs was the work of a band of "dog soldiers," gathered from various tribes and headed by Charlie Bent, the half-breed outlaw, son of Colonel William Bent. The "dog soldiers" were the worst renegades the troops had to fight against on the plains. They were Indians who had been kicked out of their villages by their own tribes for various offences. They were always more bloodthirsty, if possible, then the ordinary Indian. They were the Ishmaelites of the plains; their hands were against every man and they were as ready to attack their own people as they were to fight the pale face. There was no torture their fiendish minds could conceive that they would not carry out, laughing over their victim's agony and boasting to the poor wretch how brave their torturers were.[16]

These "dog soldiers" were never punished for killing the Hunigs. Some time afterward, when the winter set in and they decided to quit the warpath and become "good" Indians again until spring, they came into the fort to get their winter's supplies from the government and began boasting about what they had done, and saying it would only take the next summer for them to clean out every fort in the country. They never wearied of bragging of their deviltries and telling how brave they were. Many a time when they were boasting, I have made them angry by saying jeeringly:

"What—do you call yourselves brave? Bah! you are nothing but a lot of cowards! You say you are braves and then you go out and kill a lot of women and children. That is not the work of braves—it is the work of cowards! I know how you brave warriors lay your plans: fifteen or twenty of you will slip up to a house and when you see the white men leave, you know there are only women and children inside to fight you. Oh, yes; it is very brave for big bucks like you,

[15] Franz Huning tells us that upon his return the following year, he removed the bodies of his in-laws from Fort Zarah and took them to Ellsworth for reburial (Browne, *Trader on the Santa Fe Trail*, p. 93).

[16] Charlie Bent, named for his slain uncle, was the son of William Bent and his second Cheyenne wife, Yellow Woman. Young Charlie sided with his mother's people in their fierce war with the whites and became leader of a ferocious band of raiders. He narrowly escaped death at the Sand Creek Massacre in 1864. Contrary to Christy's assertion, the term Dog Soldiers did not mean a collection of renegades from assorted tribes; it referred to a prominent Cheyenne warrior society.

well armed with guns and sharp knives, to go in and kill those women who have no guns to fight you with. You kill them and take their scalps and then you go back to your lodges and have a scalp-dance. You call that being brave; but you are cowards. Those are the only kinds of scalps you get to hang to your belts, the scalps of women and children. And when you are in your lodges, safe from all danger, and with your bellies full of buffalo-meat, it is then you tell your children how brave you have been to take those scalps and you pat yourselves on the breast and sing. Bah—you are not men, you are only old squaws! Why don't you fight us white dogs face to face when you meet us? But you are only a lot of squaws. You are afraid to meet us face to face like men!''

Then I would wind up by reminding them how four of us white trappers once whipped a party of fifty Kiowas on the Little Arkansas River and put them on the run.

Whew! but they would be fighting mad! They would stride forward, shaking their fists high in the air and say:

"Never mind. We will meet you some day and then we will kill you all!''

The affair I alluded to happened on Little Cow Creek in 1860 and the Indians never forgot it. In that year Bill Matthewson had a trading-post on Little Cow Creek. Bill Matthewson was the original "Buffalo Bill.'' I have known the present one, Colonel William F. Cody, since he was fourteen years old.[17]

One day the Kiowas sent word to Matthewson that they intended to clean out his place and Bill along with it. Bill was afraid of nobody, nor of any living thing. He sent word back by the Indian courier telling the Kiowas to come on, that he was waiting for them and wanted a little fun with them anyway, and that he was ready and able and willing to kill the whole Kiowa village if only they would all come at once.

[17] William ("Buffalo Bill") Mathewson operated a trading post and served as postmaster at the Cow Creek (not Little Cow Creek) crossing on the Santa Fe Trail during the 1860s. The bridge over the creek was completed early in 1860. Historian Louise Barry, who shows that the fight with the Kiowas occurred in 1864 rather than 1860, has pointed out that Captain Christy could not have taken part, since he was then serving with the Third Illinois Cavalry in the Civil War. But she adds: "Although he could not have been in Kansas in 1864, his description is so convincing—with allowance for a little exaggeration—it would seem he must have heard the story from one of the participants" ("The Ranch at Cow Creek Crossing," *Kansas Historical Quarterly* 38 [Winter 1972]: 433).

There were only four of us at Bill's place—Hurricane Bill, Bronco Sam, Bill Matthewson and myself—but we were well armed and itching to settle old scores with the Kiowas, and every one of us felt equal to the job of killing off the whole bunch single-handed.

After the courier had gone with Bill's reply, we prepared for the coming siege. About a hundred and fifty yards above the post the creek was spanned by a bridge eight feet wide and thirty feet long. We had a six-pounder cannon which the Indians knew nothing about. We loaded the six-pounder with about a quart of minie-balls, scraps of iron and things, and trained it on the bridge. The bridge was the only approach to the post, and over it we knew the Kiowas must cross if they came. Bill then stationed himself beside the cannon and the rest of us took up positions with our carbines behind the adobe walls of the out-buildings and waited.

The next morning we were rewarded by seeing the Kiowas coming in full force, clad in war-paint and feathers and fully armed. They made no pretense of taking us by surprise but came riding along at a steady trot, yelling their war-cries and shaking their lances in the air. We kept out of sight and made no reply to their yells. In a few minutes they came streaming over the bridge in a long close line, making such beautiful targets of themselves that I could scarcely keep from jumping in the air and cracking my heels for joy.

"Bill," I cried, "hold me. I can almost see wings sprouting on some of those Indians!"

"How so, Charlie?" asked Bill.

"Oh," I said, "in a minute we will make good Indians of them and they will be angels soon!"

"Ha, ha!" laughed Bill. "All right, Charlie; now watch them fall!"

And bang! went the six-pounder.

The firing of the cannon was the first intimation they had that we were ready for them and the Indians were thrown into instant confusion. As the minie balls and scrap iron scattered among them, horses and riders fell together and were piled on the bridge in a struggling mass. The canon's discharge was followed by a volley from our carbines that brought down several more; and then we came out from behind the adobe walls and made a break toward the Indians, yelling and firing as we ran.

The surprise was complete. It needed no more to put the enemy on the run. As soon as they could recover their wits and extricate themselves from the mass of falling men and plunging horses the survivors turned and fled back across the bridge as fast as their horses could carry them, and scattered to the shelter of the hills; and those who had fallen from the bridge into the water were forced to swim or drown.

In the meantime we kept them on the run by firing at them as fast as we could; and when we quit making "good" Indians and the last live one had disappeared, our carbines were red hot. It was the most one-sided fight I ever saw. That single discharge from the six-pounder must have killed about twenty Indians, with their horses, and wounded as many more; and I am sure we killed about ten others with our carbines. The bridge and the banks of the creek were strewn with dead.

That settled the fight as far as the Kiowas were concerned. They did not come back to resume it. We saw no more of them and as the day wore on we thought they were running yet. But, about mid-afternoon, we saw three or four Indians coming afoot over the bridge. At the bridge they halted and, waving a white flag, stretched out their hands in token of peace.

We went over to see what they wanted. They were peace messengers, sent by the band, and begged Bill not to shoot. They said they did not want to fight any more; they would be good Indians now and they only wanted Bill to permit them to take their dead away. The permission was granted and the messengers returned to the top of the ridge and signaled to their comrades. They were presently joined by a group who at once began to remove the dead and wounded from where they had fallen on the bridge or along the banks of the creek, and to carry them away beyond the ridge. The Indians regard it a sacred duty to remove all of their dead who are slain in battle, and the survivors will go through great hardships and danger in order to do so. This task kept the Kiowas busy until dark; and all through the night we could hear them wailing for the dead.

The Kiowas never forgot that fight. They made peace with Bill and never bothered him again. And always after that they called him *Sympah Zilvah,* or the Strong Man.

12. José Librado Gurulé's Recollections, 1867

José Librado Gurulé's recollection of his journey over the Santa Fe Trail in 1867 is believed to be unique. At least, no other account by a native New Mexican drover has thus far come to light. That this one was recorded is almost entirely because of a happy accident.

In the depression era of the late 1930s, Mrs. Lou Sage Batchen was living in the remote Hispanic village of Las Placitas, New Mexico, located about twenty miles northeast of Albuquerque in the foothills of the Sandia Mountains. By luck she was able to obtain employment with the New Mexico Federal Writers' Project, a government program whose intention was to aid needy authors. Like other members of the project who were scattered throughout the state, she was directed to collect and record the folkways of Hispanic villagers. Over a period of several years, Mrs. Batchen produced dozens of short manuscripts based upon interviews with her neighbors.

On February 16, 1940, she took down the story of eighty-eight-year-old José Librado Gurulé, who as a lad of sixteen had gone to Missouri and back on the Santa Fe Trail.[1] Because Mrs. Batchen was a sympathetic listener and because she possessed a familiarity with the local language and customs, her recording of Gurulé's tale seems to have retained much of the flavor and authenticity of the original oral account. Hundreds of young New Mexicans like José Gurulé, of the peon class, are known to have traveled the trail as herders and retainers for wealthy merchants. But he alone, so far as we know, found someone who could set down his experiences and impressions in writing.

[1] The typescript, under the title "Over the Santa Fe Trail in 1867," is preserved in the WPA Writers' File, History Library, Museum of New Mexico, Santa Fe.

Little is known about Gurulé beyond what is recorded in his recollections. He told Mrs. Batchen that he was a direct descendant *of one of the first families of Las Placitas, which settled in the area in 1767 upon receiving a land grant from the Spanish government. One gathers that much of his life was spent in poverty. The date of his death, most probably during the 1940s, is not known.*

The owner of the wagon caravan to which Gurulé was attached was José Leandro (or Leander) Perea, a prominent merchant and sheep baron who resided in the town of Bernalillo, on the Rio Grande, a few miles west of Las Placitas. Gurulé mentions that Perea was wealthy; in fact, in his day, Perea was regarded as the richest man in New Mexico, worth some $2 million.[2] A physician named Dr. Henry F. Hoyt, who was acquainted with Perea in 1879, described him as "a man of strong character, yet he ruled over his vast domain with moderation and good judgement."[3]

From Gurulé's words, one scarcely draws a picture of Perea as being a person of moderation and sound judgment. In truth, he was an autocratic patrón *who held much of the adult male population around Bernalillo in debt peonage. When he needed drovers for one of his Missouri-bound caravans, he sent his* capitán, *or foreman, to a rural village such as Las Placitas, lined up the men and boys in the plaza, and drafted those whom he needed on the trail. The going wage for a peon in the 1860s was six to eight dollars a month. But as Gurulé points out, in this instance Perea's peons received a total of eight dollars, representing their entire wages for eleven months' work with the caravan.*

From this account a striking picture of the life of New Mexican drovers on the Santa Fe Trail emerges—the poor quality and scantiness of their native food, the exhaustion produced by over-work, the hardship, and the danger. By contrast, the conditions experienced by American bull whackers and mule skinners, as described in their own journals, seem a good deal better. But through all of this, José Gurulé appears to have remained stoic and uncomplaining, even when the dread cholera struck the returning wagon train and caused the deaths of one-third of the crew.

[2] J. H. Beadle, *The Undeveloped West; or, Five Years in the Territories* (Philadelphia: National Publishing Co., 1873), p. 489.

[3] Henry F. Hoyt, *A Frontier Doctor* (reprint, Chicago: R. R. Donnelley & Sons Co., 1979), p. 234.

Fortunate we are that he was among the survivors, for his narrative forms a valuable document in the history and lore of the trail.

It was in February, 1867, that José Gurulé, then a lad of sixteen went adventuring to Los Estados, which was the common name for Kansas City.[4]

Esquipulo Romero, El Capitán of the José Leander Perea freighting outfit, came to Las Placitas to look over Perea's men for the purpose of selecting the most able-bodied to make the annual trek over the Santa Fe Trail to Kansas City with the many thousands of pounds of wool, and then to bring back the golden returns to Perea and Nesario Gonzales, who combined their freighting but under the direction of Perea's men.[5] These two men were among the wealthy of New Mexico in their day. Perea was not only wealthy but powerful and an outstanding politician of Bernalillo County. At that time most of the men in Las Placitas were Perea's men and at his command, and all because the Perea ledger showed nearly all of them to be in his debt.

Esquipulo could tell at a glance a trail-worthy man, a man who could keep going. Youth offered possibilities for those endurance trips, for in the main that was exactly what they meant. There was husky Joaquin Trujillo, a strong and well developed man, though he was but nineteen. He was told to get ready for duty. Juan Baptiste had proven his mettle on a previous trip as had Nicolás Gurulé, so both were chosen. José Gurulé, son of Nicolás, had grit and wit and was as tough as a pine knot. He wanted to go and was taken. There

[4] *Los Estados* (the States) was the term first used by New Mexicans to refer to the head of the Santa Fe Trail. By the 1860s it had become synonymous with Kansas City, then the chief supply point for caravans.

[5] The export of wool from New Mexico to Missouri was a new phenomenon of the 1850s and 1860s. Before that time, eastbound wagons had occasionally carried a few bales of furs, but more often they traveled empty, or nearly so. Wool production on the upper Rio Grande had long been retarded because of constant Navajo attacks upon the flocks. But by 1865 a military campaign by Kit Carson had brought defeat to the tribe, and at once, sheep raising entered a period of spectacular growth. Although bulky to freight, wool brought a fair price in the East, where fibers of all classes were much in demand by New England textile mills. The surplus that quickly appeared in New Mexico provided a marketable commodity that men like Perea could use to cover the expenses of their trains to Kansas City. There, manufactured goods were purchased, and the return was made with full loads.

were others picked from among the men of Las Placitas but who they were and why they were chosen has long been forgotten.

For the journey the men needed clothing which would stay on their backs for at least three months, and shoes and *tewas*, whichever they could afford.[6] Each man must take his own bedroll. These were usually made up of serapes woven on the village looms, or home-woven Mexican blankets. The men's suits were *mantas* (drawers and shirt of coarse white cotton cloth) and underwear made of goat hair woven into cloth on the household looms. The serapes which were men's shawls sometimes served as coats but mostly the men wore coats called *cotóns*. They were woven and made on the looms by the women. That is, the material was, and it was made just as rag carpets were made. The *cotóns* were cut short to the waist line in front and were long, nearly to the knees behind. They were fastened in front with wooden buttons. These coats were very warm.

But the greatest preparations for the trip went on in the cook-house of the José Leander Perea place in Bernalillo. There tortillas were made by the hundreds and packed away. Bushels of dried peas were finely ground between stones to make "coffee." Huge quantities of mutton and goat meat, onions, frijoles, black eyed peas (alike in taste but smaller in size than the black eyed peas of today), and chili were amassed. All meat was dried. These supplies were put away in the rolling commissary from which Esquipulo dispensed meals daily. Besides each man was allotted a limited quantity of cube sugar and some tobacco, which he carried with him. The tobacco was called *punche* because that was the name of a wild plant they cut and dried and used in their cigarettes. Then to better the quality of this "tobacco" some cultivated the plant. It was this *punche* that was taken on the trip in 1867. Most if not all of the men carried some of the wild *punche* with them in a bottle-shaped container made of ox hide and sewed with thongs of the same hide, and they had a cork made of wood. These were called *guajetes* (a Mexican word). The men also carried with them a pack of corn husks prepared for them by their women at home. The husks were properly dried and soaked

[6] *Tewas* were distinctive leather moccasins made and worn by the Indians of the Southwest and much favored by the poorer class among their Hispanic neighbors (see Marc Simmons, "Footwear on New Mexico's Hispanic Frontier," in *Southwestern Culture History,* ed. Charles H. Lange, [Santa Fe, N.Mex.: Ancient City Press, 1985], pp. 223–31).

and cut into pieces which would make the cigarettes about six inches long. They laid them in neat packs, enough for the journey, and wrapped them with a square of deer or goat hide and tied the pack with a string of hide.

At the appointed time some ten wagons which would form a part of the Perea-Gonzales train rumbled through Placitas. Heavy wagons loaded with wool, each of them drawn by five spans of oxen; for the roads were heavy with mud, especially on the *plana* (level ground). In February or early spring, when the wagons left for Los Estados, the road through the village and on toward Tejón was a popular route. The men at Las Placitas joined the procession as it passed through. The route was through Tejón Cañon, in all probability one of the ancient trails in New Mexico. In the region of San Pedro Mountains, which is a relatively short distance from Tejón Cañon, is the ruin of San Pedro Viejo, an early pueblo. Across the Rio Grande at Bernalillo is an old pueblo now being restored. Tejón Cañon is part of a natural road between these places.

But to get back on the trail. When the wagons rattled through the gate of the town of Tejón the villagers swarmed about them, saying farewells and wishing their friends a safe journey. Some accompanied the expedition as far as Golden, the next village. They trudged along with the men who were using their long sticks skillfully to keep the oxen plodding along and in order.[7] From Golden the train swung to a northerly direction, but that was after a night spent somewhere near that place. The next village on the route was Cerrillos, then Galisteo. They continued toward Glorieta until night, when they camped. The route through the mountains was difficult and progress slow, for the snow was deep, but at length they passed through Glorieta and headed for Las Vegas.[8]

Las Vegas was the starting point of the big adventure as well as the meeting place for those who wished to add their wagons and *carretas* to the train.[9] The remainder of the wagons and oxen and

[7] Mexican drovers controlled their oxen with goads—long pointed sticks—in contrast to American bull whackers, who used a "black snake," or a whip with a popper at the end.

[8] The branch trail that led in a northeasterly direction from Bernalillo, Las Placitas, and Galisteo joined the main Santa Fe Trail about fifteen miles east of Santa Fe, near the western end of Glorieta Pass.

[9] *Carretas* were cumbersome two-wheeled carts made entirely of wood. Gregg speaks of seeing them in use along the Cimarron Cut-off (*Commerce of the Prairies,*

mules which were to make up the Perea-Gonzales train, and which had come by various routes to Las Vegas (depending upon what part of the Rio Grande Valley or surrounding montains they were in when the drive started) were there with all the others from other parts of the territory who wished to join the caravan. There were about four hundred carriers in all besides the herds of mules and oxen being driven along to take the place of the animals that happened to fall by the way.

In organizing for the trip each outfit held its own place in the caravan. The Perea-Gonzales layout was well in the lead with its fifty wagons or more of various sizes. Wagons piled high with wool, feed for the mules and oxen, the commissary, wagons loaded with firewood and small barrels filled with water to be used where such necessities were not to be found. The barrels were refilled wherever water was found. No man in the outfit was without his *guaje* (Mexican word and meaning a long-neck gourd) which he carried with him as he went along and drank sparingly from it frequently or moistened his lips. These were refilled from every watering place they came upon. In taking wood and water with them much time was saved. On these trips to the wool market time was important.

About the middle of February the caravan started. At Las Vegas there was nothing to mark the momentous event but behind them in every home from which these men had come to venture upon the long and dangerous voyage, simple but impressive ceremonies were held. In every home candles were lit before favorite saints and prayers were offered. Then the wives or mothers of the departed men wrapped a cloth about the saints supplicated and put them in captivity to hold them there as hostages for the safe return of their men. The bottom of the homemade chest, which was an article of furniture in every house, became the prison of the saints. When the men came back the saints in those homes were resurrected and a wake held in their honor and there was dancing and singing. In those houses where the men did not return, the saints were taken from captivity and buried with sad and solemn ceremony. In the absence of wife or mother any adult member of the household conducted the ceremonies.

pp. 67, 147). For a description of their construction see Marc Simmons, ''Carros y Carretas: Vehicular Traffic on the Camino Real,'' in *Hispanic Arts and Ethnohistory in the Southwest,* ed. Marta Weigle (Santa Fe, N.Mex.: Ancient City Press, 1983), pp. 325–34.

José Librado Aron Gurulé said that the trail taken by the
caravan was the one called a short cut and made by Aubry, and that
at the beginning it was like a great ranch. In those days the poorer
native New Mexicans knew no English and they had their own way
of interpreting English names they heard. From his description of
the route it was doubtless the one followed and outlined by Gregg.[10]
Lemita was the last settlement in New Mexico they passed
before going into Kansas, José said.[11] They went along the Cimarron Route to the Arkansas River. They crossed the Cimarron "at the
best crossing," which must have been what was known on the Old
Trail as Middle Spring.[12] From the beginning of the march both men
and animals were pushed to the limit. A schedule was set and every
effort made to maintain it. The drive was kept as near a continuous
eighteen hours as was possible. The halt came at ten in the morning
or as near that time as could be managed. There was a rush and
bustle to get the animals unhooked from the wagons, to feed the men
and the beasts and get in some sleep in the allotted time. Before the
last lap of the Cimarron Trail was reached the animals were so
exhausted that they almost dropped when released from the wagons.
Within six hours of the halting moment the train was again in
motion. This order was not relaxed until after the Cimarron was
crossed. Then there was much less danger of attacks by the Indians.
In traveling all night they could not break camp in the mornings and
find themselves surrounded by the enemy. Maintaining the eighteen
hour travel schedule and not the driving through the nights was to

[10] Here Mrs. Batchen inserts an interpretive comment: that is, the Aubry Cut-off
was "doubtless the one followed and outlined by Gregg." But she is in error.
Gurulé's caravan began by following the Cimarron Cut-off through northeastern New
Mexico (the route familiar to Gregg). Near Cold Springs in the Oklahoma Panhandle,
however, it veered off the main trail and picked up the so-called Aubry Route, which
led in a more direct line northeast to the Arkansas River, where it joined the Mountain
Branch a few miles east of present-day Syracuse, Kansas. That shortcut was
pioneered and opened by freighter Francis X. Aubry in 1851 (Leo E. Oliva, "The
Aubry Route of the Santa Fe Trail," *Kansas Quarterly* 5 [Spring 1973]: 18–29; and
Eugene P. Burr, *A Detailed Study of the Aubry Cutoff of the Santa Fe Trail and Fort
Aubry*, Research Studies [Emporia: Emporia Kansas State College, 1974]).

[11] The location of Lemita—the Spanish word for buckbrush—has not been
established.

[12] Here again Mrs. Batchen was guessing as to the route. Since the caravan had
taken the Aubry Cut-off, it would have left the Cimarron Valley long before reaching
Middle Spring, a famous landmark close to the river and about eight miles north of
present-day Elkhart, Kansas.

blame for weakened condition of both men and beasts. That was an unjustifiable hardship.

In making the one stop in the twenty-four hours the scouts looked for camping grounds where there were no signs of prairie dogs. That meant that the area would be absolutely barren of vegetation and no fires could menace them; which was another safeguard against the raiding Indians. Often the whole caravan was raced in order to reach such a place. The men who guided the oxen with their long goads must run to keep the pace. There was but one full meal during each twenty-four hours. It was supplemented by two light snacks; the first consisting of a tortilla and an onion in the hand to be eaten on the run; the second, an onion and a tortilla eaten likewise. The men were drawing heavily upon previously stored up energy. This army of hirelings was traveling on its feet with very little assistance from its stomach, according to the picture painted of it by one who endured the experience and related it. And as for rest or recreation, there was none.[13] The stops made on the entire trip were too short to permit such indulgences. The halts were purely business matters made for the purpose of feeding and getting snatches of sleep. José said when they slept at mid-day their sleep was broken each day at twelve o'clock by the braying of the mules in the train. The men referred to them as clocks.

One afternoon a near panic was created in the Perea-Gonzales section of the caravan. Frightened oxen brought a heavily loaded wagon to a tipsy angle. The wagons and animals following were brought to an abrupt stop. An exhausted man who had stretched himself upon the tongue of the wagon preceding the one tip-tilted by the frightened oxen, had fallen into a deep sleep and rolled off to the ground. He was trampled to death before he could be rescued. A solemn pause was made while the victim was buried. This tragedy

[13] As a matter of record, other New Mexican caravans did not find it necessary to keep such a madcap pace, and there was time for storytelling and singing by troubadours around the evening campfire. For reference to contests between troubadours of rival wagon trains see Arthur L. Campa, *Hispanic Culture in the Southwest* (Norman: University of Oklahoma Press, 1979), p. 240. It should be noted that some American trail journals also referred to excessive fatigue and spoke of men going to sleep on the wagon tongue. Charles Raber, while crossing the plains in the 1860s, wrote: "The most trouble we had was to keep the men from riding on the wagon tongues during the night; they would go to sleep and fall off, thus getting run over" ("Personal Recollections of Life on the Plains from 1860 to 1868," *Westport Historical Quarterly* 7 [Mar., 1972]: 11).

happened in other outfits on that journey. Under the strain of eighteen hour marches the men were giving way. "Too much awake. Too little water to drink, too little frijoles; men go to sleep anywhere," was the comment of the narrator.

One morning when they halted to make ready to cross El Arroyo Grande (the Big Arroyo) and which they later learned was the Arkansas River, they sighted on the plains coming toward them a band of Indians. Indians on the march. There was a hasty conference among the captains of the caravan. There was excited talk and anxiety among all the others in the train. On came the Indian band, looming large and ominous in the distance. Nearer they came. The order went out from the captains not to fire or make a move until word came from the proper authority. But as the band bore down upon them the ordeal of waiting proved too much for a few near the point of approach. They fired. At once the fire was returned and one man near the Perea-Gonzales outfit went down. For a moment it looked as if the situation was out of hand. But Esquipulo and a few other courageous ones stepped forward and made signs of friendship to the Indians. At that all appearances of hostility vanished and the band advanced. Some were on foot, a few rode mules, some drove mules hitched to queer looking conveyances built exactly like ladders; two stout poles with strong cross pieces. One end of the ladder was harnessed to the mule, the other dragged the ground.[14] Bundles, pots, small articles of wearing apparel, and a lot of little things (José said he never saw anything like them before and what he dubbed *junco* junk was tied to the poles and dangled down). Women and children sat on the cross pieces of the ladders as if on seats in a wagon. Many of the Indians rode horses, the prizes for which they would murder and plunder. Luckily, the caravan boasted no horses, and there was a reason. It made the trips less hazardous in cases like the one they were experiencing. The train contained little to tempt the Indians on the east bound trip.

One old woman drove her mule and ladder close to the spot where José Gurulé was standing. She dismounted and approached him, her eyes upon the cube of sugar he held untasted in his hand. He sensed her desire and at once took another cube from the scanty hoard in his pocket and gave the two to her. She thanked him, or he supposed that was what she said; for he had no understanding of her

---

[14] José's "ladder" was the common travois of the Plains Indians.

language. Then she went to her ladder and untied a bundle. From it she took a pat of ground meat and came back and gave it to him. He thanked her in his own language. She smiled, returned to her seat on the top cross piece of the ladder, and took up her lines.

In time the band passed peacefully on its way, bound for Fort Dodge, *Fuerte Doche* they called it. *Fuerte* (strong) suggested by the place being a fort; *Doche* being their own interpretation of Dodge. The Indians were going there to receive "gifts" as José said, then explained that it was rations from the United States Government. On the remainder of the caravan's journey to Kansas City, José Gurulé was the butt of many jokes. The old Indian women was referred to as his sweetheart who had come so far to bring him some choice meat, and as his grandmother who had come to see him, and seeing how hungry he looked gave him her meat.

Before the end of the journey out of the vast plains, one small place José called and spelled "Napeste" attracted their attention. It was a very small post office and it was under guard. He did not remember why they called it a post office, nor why it was guarded, if he ever knew. As a railroad was being built through that place he thought it might have something to do with that.[15]

At last the caravan rolled into the appointed grounds in Kansas City and on time, that is, they made it in three months. Then more work for the men; unloading and carting wool to storage and conditioning the mules, oxen, and wagons for the homeward trip. On the first day of their arrival some of the men wandered idly from the camping grounds. They walked along hoping to see wonderful sights. The very first thing which met their eyes was a huge, bright-colored picture of an Indian on the front of a wooden building. He was wearing a war bonnet. The words under the Indian read,

[15] From at least the early eighteenth century, the Spaniards knew the Arkansas River as the Rio Napeste or Napestle. Doubtless, it was an Indian word, but its origin is uncertain. One theory is that it is the Comanche term for a "platform burial." In the Big Timbers, along the river in eastern Colorado, the Indians were in the habit of cutting wood to construct their mortuary platforms. Travelers on the Santa Fe Trail occasionally mentioned seeing these curious "burials." Other sources claim that Napeste is derived from the Osage words *ne shusta*, which mean red water (Ralph C. Taylor, *Colorado, South of the Border* [Denver, Colo.: Sage Books, 1963], p. 19). The early French explorers called the river Arcansas or Acansas, from which comes Arkansas.

TOMASITO THE FAMOUS WARRIOR OF THE FAMED VILLAGE OF TAOS.
"We all laughed," José said, "to find Tomasito in Los Estados."[16]
After enjoying the colorful likeness of the Taos Warrior, they wandered on. They heard a welcome sound. It was music, and they hurried on to find it. It was the first sound of music they had heard since they left Las Placitas. They almost danced along, José said. (The men with him on this sightseeing venture were all from Las Placitas.) But never had they heard such music as this. It was a Negro band and they were all dressed up in white coat and pants and tall black hats. They played outside a place where there was a minstrel show. The men had no money with which to buy tickets to go in, so they just stood around and listened. José carried money enough to pay for a worsted suit out of a store and nothing could tempt him to part with one penny of it. He had boasted around Las Placitas that he would bring back a suit of clothes from Kansas City and he had sold some of his goats to get the money.

The stay in Kansas City was short. Too soon Esquipulo checked them over to find who needed clothes and shoes to start back. He found most of the men in tatters and outfitted them with new *mantas* made after the same pattern as those they had worn on the long trip. "Linens" they were called in Los Estados and listed as such in the Perea books where they were charged for "linens" and not *mantas*. Everyone in the outfit needed shoes, another item to enter in the Perea accounts to be paid for in due course in labor imposed by Esquipulo or others in charge of the Perea interests.

Once again the train was on the march, but westward now. Wagons were loaded with merchandise of every description. There were copper kettles and there were pans and pots and dishes of china and plated and steel wear for table use and many bolts and bundles of cloth and there were hats for women and men and shoes; all these to be put into the Perea store at Bernalillo. Many wagons were loaded with food supplies. Little did the men who goaded the oxen, drove the mules, herded along the animals to replace the fallen beasts, and otherwise met the gruelling demands of the trip know what awaited them. The time was June, the days were moist, windy, and blazing

[16] Tomasito of Taos Pueblo was a leader of the Indian and Mexican rebels who killed Gov. Charles Bent and other Americans in the uprising of January, 1847. The following month he was slain in battle by United States forces which marched north from Santa Fe to put down the disturbance.

hot. At Great Bend in Kansas the Perea-Gonzales band dropped out of the caravan. They traveled in a northerly direction for three days. They came upon Fort Hays garrisoned by Negro soldiers. There they saw a few Negro women, the only women they saw anywhere on the trail. There was no stop at the fort, they passed on to Hays City where the new railroad, the Kansas Pacific was laying track under the protection of the soldiers at the fort. The protection was as necessary as the timber and iron in the construction of the railroad. All about the new railroad town of Hays City were resentful, hostile Indians. And it was at this spot that the caravan halted. Perea and Gonzales had taken a contract to furnish wagons, teams, and men to work on this railroad that was being built across the state.

A rough camp was set up and everything put in readiness for the cook. That was important; what he dished out to the men was to be the tie that bound them to the job. The commissary was well stocked with real coffee, enough sugar cubes for all, white flour for bread once a day, and butter to spread on it. There was ham and bacon and there would be fresh meat. It was to be a delectable handout three times a day.

Men and animals went to work. For a time the new and hitherto unsampled food and the shifting scenes about them kept the native New Mexicans going their placid ways. But soon there was distress in camp. The hard, unaccustomed manual labor was taking its toll of strength. They worked along with the other laborers who were mostly ''Anglos'' which meant that they were white men. Other than that José Gurulé could not name their nationality. There were some Negroes on the job. All of these men could stand the heat better than the New Mexicans. No one living all his days in the mountains of New Mexico could sleep during the hot, blistering July nights in Kansas. The water was disagreeable, the food remained good in quality but dwindled in quantity. Men were worn thin, but kept on their feet. Men and animals were driven to the point of exhaustion, but the contract must be fulfilled.

But at last it was over and again the Perea-Gonzales outfit turned westward. The wagons emptied of supplies by the camp during the work were reloaded with supplies transported to Esquipulo from Kansas City to Hays City by railroad. It was on the return trip that they sighted scarcely any buffalo. A scattered few and only one was within rifle range. Someone who owned a gun fired at the lone animal and he fell. That one was José Montaño. The animal no sooner dropped than José was on top of him. To the surprise of José and all those who saw it, the buffalo leaped up and bolted forward. The man on his back could do nothing but grab the animal's long hair and cling to his back for dear life. It was nearly twenty minutes before some sign of weakness was seen in the buffalo. He was staggering; the lead José Montaño had sent into his body bringing him down. José was saved. The buffalo had galloped about a thousand yards. He was butchered and taken along as the caravan marched on. That was the only excitement on the return trip. The remainder of the trip was a nightmare. The men became weak and ill, the animals dropped. But when they fell by the way there were mules and oxen enough in the herd to replace them.

And then what José Gurulé called a "plague" broke out among them. It was called cholera. At first those who went down with it were laid in the wagons, those who stayed on foot kept the caravan moving. They just crept along. Then so many of them were down that the train was halted at Cold Spring, José Gurulé said. There they were doctored. The men were given water with plenty of whiskey and chili in it. The whiskey came from the stock being brought from Kansas City to Perea. It was Penguin. (Good corn whiskey, José said.) But somehow it did not cure the cholera, and the New Mexico chili failed them. After a halt of twelve days they moved on with hardly men enough on foot to keep the caravan moving. They made frequent short stops just to rest. There were other stops made, and always after those they left one of their number behind under a mound of earth. Many died of the plague, José said.

It was December before what was left of the Perea-Gonzales outfit dragged into Las Vegas. "A dejected looking outfit," said the story teller, "with maybe a third of it left somewhere on the way." In another week they were back in Bernalillo.

The entire trip had consumed almost eleven months. Each man who survived it was paid eight dollars in cash. The food they had eaten in the railroad camp was pay for their labor done in the railroad construction work. It was not known whether the families of the men who died on the way received any part of the eight dollars. None of the Las Placitas men was stricken by the plague it seemed, and each one of them received the eight dollars, the sum total for the eleven months plus the food at the railroad camp. But the rejoicing at home, the resurrection of the saints from the bottoms of the chests, the feasts and the *bailes* (dances)—not to mention the wine made in their absence and saved for the occasion—was a rich compensation in itself for the hardships that were now in the dead past.

José Gurulé was a man of seventeen when he reached home. And he made good his boast. He brought home a suit of worsted from Los Estados and donned it for the admiration of the whole village. It was the first suit of clothes ever worn in Las Placitas.

Appendix A. To Santa Fe via the Cimarron Cut-off

This table of major place-names on the trail between Independence and Santa Fe is based largely upon the 1848 compilation by John A. Bingham, a traveler.[1] Some additions have been made, drawing from the briefer but better-known listing prepared by Josiah Gregg for his 1844 book *Commerce of the Prairies*. Because there were many variations in the trail and because mileage figures were often merely estimates, contemporary accounts seldom agree on the distances between campsites.[2]

From	To	Miles
Missouri River	Independence	4
Independence	state line	17
state line	Lone Elm (also called Round Grove)	15
Lone Elm	Bull Creek	8
Bull Creek	Black Jack (Narrows)	15
Black Jack	Willow Spring	10
Willow Spring	110 Mile Creek	25
110 Mile Creek	Bridge (or Switzler's) Creek	10
Bridge Creek	Bluff Creek	25
Bluff Creek	Big John Spring	8
Big John Spring	Council Grove	2
Council Grove	Elm Creek	7
Elm Creek	Diamond Spring	8
Diamond Spring	Lost Spring	15
Lost Spring	Cottonwood Creek	13
Cottonwood Creek	Turkey Creek	24
Turkey Creek	Little Arkansas Crossing	20

[1] Nicholas P. Hardeman, ed., "Camp Sites on the Santa Fe Trail in 1848," *Arizona and the West* 6 (1964): 313–19.

[2] Gregg, *Commerce of the Prairies*, p. 217. Another useful itinerary appears in Alphonso Wetmore, *Gazetteer of the State of Missouri* (St. Louis, Mo.: C. Keemle, 1837), pp. 269–70.

Little Arkansas Crossing	Big Owl Creek	12
Big Owl Creek	Little Owl Creek	4
Little Owl Creek	Cow Creek	8
Cow Creek	Plum Buttes	9
Plum Buttes	Big Bend of Arkansas	7
Big Bend of Arkansas	Walnut Creek	8
Walnut Creek	Pawnee Rock	15
Pawnee Rock	Ash Creek	5
Ash Creek	Pawnee Fork	5
Pawnee Fork	Coon Creek	10
Coon Creek	Mann's Fort	52
Mann's Fort	crossing of Arkansas	30
crossing of Arkansas	Sand Creek	50
Sand Creek	Lower Springs	12
Lower Springs	Middle Spring	30
Middle Spring	Upper (or Flag) Spring	35
Upper Spring	Cold Springs	18
Cold Springs	Cedar Creek	12
Cedar Creek	McNees Creek	10
McNees Creek	Cottonwood (Alamo) Springs	10
Cottonwood (Alamo) Springs	Rabbit Ears Creek	10
Rabbit Ears Creek	Round Mound	8
Round Mound	Rock Creek	10
Rock Creek	Whetstone Creek	10
Whetstone Creek	Point of Rocks	10
Point of Rocks	Red (Canadian) River	25
Red (Canadian) River	Ocaté Creek	6
Ocaté Creek	Wagon Mound (Santa Clara Spring)	16
Wagon Mound (Santa Clara Spring)	Wolf Creek	12
Wolf Creek	Mora River (La Junta)	6
Mora River (La Junta)	Las Vegas	18
Las Vegas	Tecolote	10
Tecolote	Bernal Spring	6
Bernal Spring	San Miguel	6
San Miguel	Pecos Church	18
Pecos Church	Rock Corral	13
Rock Corral	Santa Fe	10

Appendix B. To Santa Fe via the Bent's Fort Route

The following campsites and landmarks on the Bent's Fort, or Mountain Branch, of the Santa Fe Trail are listed in sequence (without mileages) beginning with the Upper Arkansas crossing near present-day Lakin, Kansas.

Upper Arkansas crossing
Chouteau's Island
Aubry Cut-off
Big Timbers (Colorado)
Bent's New Fort and Old Fort Lyon
New Fort Lyon
Bent's Old Fort and Arkansas ford
Timpas Creek
Hole-in-the-Rock
Hole-in-the-Prairie
Trinidad
Summit of Raton Pass
Willow Springs (New Mexico)
Clifton House, on the Canadian
Rayado
Upper Ocaté crossing
Fort Union
Mora River–La Junta (here the Cimarron Cut-off and the Mountain Branch reunite)

Recommended Readings

The literature of the trail is vast, as indicated by the standard descriptive work on the subject, Jack D. Rittenhouse's *The Santa Fe Trail: A Historical Bibliography* (Albuquerque: University of New Mexico Press, 1971), which lists 718 titles. An excellent general survey remains the old but still useful R. L. Duffus, *The Santa Fe Trail* (New York: Longmans, Green & Co., 1931). More accessible, in that it is currently in print in paperback, is the scholarly but readable Seymour V. Connor and Jimmy M. Skaggs, *Broadcloth and Britches: The Santa Fe Trade* (College Station: Texas A & M University Press, 1977). A popular work that will entertain the general reader is Stanley Vestal, *The Old Santa Fe Trail* (Boston: Houghton Mifflin, 1939).

An excellent, well-researched study is Larry M. Beachum, *William Becknell, Father of the Santa Fe Trade* (El Paso: Texas Western Press, 1982). Firsthand accounts by early participants in the overland trade include John E. Sunder, ed., *Matt Field on the Santa Fe Trail* (Norman: University of Oklahoma Press, 1960); David J. Weber, ed., *Albert Pike: Prose Sketches and Poems* (Albuquerque: University of New Mexico Press, 1967); and Josiah Gregg, *Commerce of the Prairies* (Norman: University of Oklahoma Press, 1954). Basic also is Otis E. Young, *The First Military Escort on the Santa Fe Trail, 1829* (Glendale, Calif.: Arthur H. Clark Co., 1952).

Books treating special trail topics are numerous. One good example is Thomas B. Hall, *Medicine on the Santa Fe Trail* (Dayton, Ohio: Morningside Bookshop, 1971). The two best-known accounts by women travelers are Stella M. Drumm, ed., *Down the Santa Fe Trail and into Mexico: The Diary of Susan Shelby Magoffin, 1846-1847* (New Haven, Conn.: Yale University Press, 1962); and Garnet M. Brayer, ed., *Land of Enchantment: Memoirs of Marian Russell along the Santa Fe Trail* (reprint; Albuquerque: University of New Mexico Press, 1981). Often overlooked is the brief but intriguing narrative of a young woman from Emporia, Kansas, who followed the Mountain Branch as far as Bent's Fort on her way to the Colorado gold fields: Julia Archibald Holmes, *A Bloomer Girl on Pike's Peak, 1858* (Denver, Colo.: Denver Public Library, 1949).

A fine biography of a major trail figure is Donald Chaput, *Francois X. Aubry, Trader, Trailmaker and Voyageur in the Southwest, 1846-1854*

(Glendale, Calif.: Arthur H. Clark Co., 1975). Recommended as well is David K. Strate, ed., *West by Southwest: Letters of Joseph Pratt Allyn, a Traveller along the Santa Fe Trail, 1863* (Dodge City: Kansas Heritage Center, 1984).

The major forts on the trail, with the exception of Fort Lyon, have received detailed treatment in individual studies: George Walton, *Sentinel of the Plains: Fort Leavenworth and the American West* (Englewood Cliffs, N.J.: Prentice-Hall, 1973); Leo E. Oliva, *Fort Larned on the Santa Fe Trail* (Topeka: Kansas State Historical Society, 1982); David Kay Strate, *Sentinel to the Cimarron: The Frontier Experience of Fort Dodge, Kansas* (Dodge City, Kans.: Cultural Heritage and Arts Center, 1970); David Lavender, *Bent's Fort* (Lincoln: University of Nebraska Press, 1954); and Chris Emmett, *Fort Union and the Winning of the Southwest* (Norman: University of Oklahoma Press, 1965). For an overview of United States military activities see Leo E. Oliva, *Soldiers on the Santa Fe Trail* (Norman: University of Oklahoma Press, 1967).

Those who wish to retrace the trail today will find these two books helpful: Hobart E. Stocking, *The Road to Santa Fe* (New York: Hastings House, 1971); and Marc Simmons, *Following the Santa Fe Trail: A Guide for Modern Travelers,* rev. ed. (Santa Fe, N.Mex.: Ancient City Press, 1986).

Index

abolitionists in Kansas, 54
Albuquerque, N.Mex., 71, 75, 112
Alexander, G. M., 37, 39, 42, 43, 44
  shoots prairie dog, 46
  shoots antelope, 48, 49
Allison, William, 57 n.9
Alvarez, Manuel
  as U.S. consul, 3
  escapes assassination, 7
  Mexico refuses to recognize, 7
  Armijo refuses passport for, 8
  report of, 8–10
  encounters snowstorm, 14
American Political party, 57 n.8
Anderson, Clinton P. (senator), 20
Anderson, Paul, Jr., 14
Anderson, William, Sr., 14
antelope, 62, 80, 82, 93
  hunting and cooking of, 48, 49, 69
Apaches, 19, 20, 29, 35
  See also Mescalero Apaches
Arapahos, 29, 35, 53, 59, 62
  their villages described, 60–61
  and massacre at Plum Buttes, 108
Arkansas River, 12, 13, 14, 24, 25,
  30, 32, 35 n.5, 47 n.6, 53, 57, 59,
  61, 62, 70, 71, 80, 93, 94, 98,
  99, 101, 104, 105, 106, 111, 112,
  126, 128, 129
  See also Little Arkansas River
Arkansas Valley, 30, 69
Armijo, Manuel, 7, 8, 9, 15 n.19
Armstrong, Maj. William F., 100
Ash Creek, 23, 24
Atkinson, Col. Henry, 59 n.11
Aubry, Francis X., 25, 126 n.10
Aubry, Mount, 35

Aubry Cut-off, 25, 35 n.5, 98, 99, 105,
  126 n.10
Autobees (Otterby), Charles, 62 n.14

Baird, James, 14
Baldwin City, Kans., 54
Baptiste, Juan, 122
barouche, described, 107 n.3
Batchen, Mrs. Lou Sage, 120
Bear Creek, 25
Becknell, William, 1
Bent, Charley, 61, 116, 130 n.16
Bent, Mollie, 61
Bent, William, 59, 61, 116
Bent, Mrs. William, 61
Bentrup, Paul, v
Bent's New Fort, 53, 61, 99
Bent's Old Fort, 53, 59, 61, 70, 98,
  104
Bernalillo, N.Mex., 121, 124, 130,
  132
Bernal Spring, 102
Betts, Amelia, v
Bible, 85, 94
Biddle, C. S., 18, 19, 20
Big Bend. See Great Bend of Arkansas
  River
Big John Creek, 78 n.8
Big Timbers (in eastern Colorado),
  129 n.15
Big Turkey Creek, 22
Bingham, John A., 135
Black Jack, Battle of, 52, 54
"black snake" (whip with popper at
  end), 124 n.7
blizzards. See storms on the Santa Fe
  Trail

Boiling Fountain Creek (Fontaine Que
  Bouille), 62, 63, 104
Boone, Daniel, 38, 53, 57
Boone, George Hampton, 38, 53
Boone, Hampton L., 38, 53, 57
Boothe, Francis, 57n.9
Border Ruffians, 54n.6
Border Times, The (Westport, Mo.), 54
Bosque Redondo Reservation, 20
Boyse, Louis, 41, 42, 43, 44, 45, 47,
  48
Brake, Hezekiah
  his wife and daughter, 37, 39
  picture of, 38
  wolf steals his boot and bridle, 38,
    49
  narrative by, 39–51
  cooks prairie dog, 47
  cooks antelope, 48, 49
Brake, Lizzie, 37, 39, 45
Brannon, Bill, 57
Bronco Sam, 118
Brown, James, 15n.12, 16n.13
Brown, John, 52, 54, 55
Brown, Russell and Company, 15
buffalo, 61
  calf's head cooked, 18, 23
  herds of, sighted, 23, 24, 59, 68,
    80, 93, 131–32
  hunting of, 23, 53, 55, 56, 57, 132
  chips, used as fuel, 41, 45, 46, 47,
    48, 55, 57, 67, 89, 101, 105
  dried meat of, as food, 55, 79
Buffalo Bill's Well, picture of freight
  wagons at, 56
buffalo dance, 21
Buford, Col. Jefferson, 54n.7
Buford's Men, 54
Bull Creek, 68
bull whackers, 75, 84, 87, 88, 90, 92,
  93, 95, 121, 124n.7
Burlingame, Kans., 41, 68, 101
Burwell, Mrs. M. T., Jr., 65

Caddo Station, Indian Terr., 87
Calhoun, James S., 11
California, 4, 29, 73
Camp (Fort) Nichols, 4, 81n.12,
  100n.8
Canadian (Colorado; Red) River, 82,
  99, 103

Carleton, Gen. Henry, 20
Carleton, Maj. James H., 11
carretas (carts), 124n.9
Carson, Christopher ("Kit"), 38, 64,
  81n.12, 100, 122n.5
Casa Depallo (Upper Cimarron or
  Flag) Spring, 80, 81n.11
Cassidy, Gerald, ii
cavallard (or cavyard; cavvy), 69, 89
Caws. See Kaws
Cedar Bluffs, 100
Cedar Springs, 81
Cerrillos, N.Mex., 124
Chambers, Samuel, 14
Chase, Kans., Santa Fe Trail wheel
  ruts near, 110
Chávez (Chauvey), Antonio José,
  68n.6
Cherokees, 62
Cheyennes, 32, 34, 38, 41, 46, 53, 58,
  61, 94, 106
  and massacre at Plum Buttes, 108,
    112
  Dog Soldiers of, 116n.16
Chihuahua, Mex., 12, 15, 68n.6
cholera, 121, 132
Chouteau's Island, 13, 14, 35n.5, 98,
  105
Chouteau's Mound (Indian Mound),
  35n.5
Christy, Capt. Charles, 106, 108, 110
  on James Fenimore Cooper, 4, 111
  memoirs of, 111–19
  on Indians, 111, 116
  fights Kiowas at Little Cow Creek,
    118–19
Cimarron (village), 103
Cimarron Crossing, 71, 99, 100
Cimarron Cut-off, 12, 47n.6, 50n.7,
  75, 97n.2, 124n.9, 126n.10
Cimmaron River, 12, 15, 25, 26, 35,
  47n.6, 48, 80n.10, 99, 100, 103
Cimmaron Route, 70, 71, 98, 99, 126
Civil War, 15, 39, 65, 66, 67, 72, 75,
  84, 96, 112
Clay, Cassius M., 57n.8
Cody, Col. William F. ("Buffalo
  Bill"), 117n.17
Cold Spring, 51, 81, 126n.10, 132
Collins, James L., 8, 12
  his report on winter travel, 13–17

Colorado
    Santa Fe Trail in, 2
    discovery of gold in, 52, 73
Colorado Chiquito (Little Colorado, or
    Cimarron), 103
Colorado (Canadian) River, 82
Colt bowie knives, 29
Colt revolvers, 29
Comanches, 30, 58
    burial platforms of, 129 n.15
comet, seen by Kellogg in 1858, 55
Commerce of the Prairies (J. Gregg), 8
Confederates, 70, 75, 96
Congress, 16
    and proposals for protection along
        Santa Fe Trail, 13, 17
Connelly, Dr. Henry, 14, 15 n.9
cooking
    of buffalo calf's head, 18, 23
    of prairie dogs, 47
    of antelope, elk, 48, 49, 69
    of rabbits, 69
    of buffalo, 69
    in preparation for trail trip, 123
Cooper, James Fenimore, 4, 111
cotons (coats), 123
Cottonwood Creek, 7–8, 14, 16, 21,
    26, 55, 68
Cottonwood Fork, 9, 10
Council Grove, Kans., 14, 21, 26, 37,
    39, 40, 41, 42, 51, 55, 61, 68,
    78, 84, 88, 91, 101
Cow Creek, 42, 55, 68, 79, 91, 101,
    108, 110
    See also Little Cow Creek
Cow Creek Crossing, 56
coyotes, 69, 93
Craig's Ranch, 104
Cripple Creek, Colo., 85
Custer, Lt. Col. George Armstrong,
    106

deer, 93
Desert Route, 25
Devil's Backbone, 50 n.7, 51
Diamond Springs (Kans.), 42, 68, 79,
    84, 88, 91
Dodge City, Kans., 11, 14, 59, 70
Dog Soldiers (Cheyenne warrior soci-
    ety), 116 n.16
Doniphan, Col. Alexander W., 68 n.4
Doniphan Expedition, 68

ducks, 22
Dunn, Captain, 54 n.7

Easton, Kans., 67
El Arroyo Grande (Big Arroyo, or
    Arkansas River), 128
elk, 69
Elkins, Stephen B., 20
Elm Creek, 55
Emancipation Proclamation, 66
End of the Trail, The (painting by
    Gerald Cassidy), frontispiece

Faulkner. See Fouglin, John
Fergusson, Clara Huning, 76 n.5
Fergusson, Harvey, 75, 108, 109
Fillmore, Millard, 11, 19
Flag Spring (Upper Cimarron Spring),
    80, 81 n.11
Fontaine Que Bouille (Boiling Fountain
    Creek), 62, 63, 104
Fort Atkinson (or Fort Mann, Kans.),
    11, 16, 24, 26, 59
Fort Aubry (Kans.), 4, 101 n.9
Fort Bent (Colo.), 36, 91, 94
    See also Bent's New Fort; Bent's
    Old Fort
Fort Dodge (Kans.), 4, 35, 79, 97 n.2,
    100, 101, 105, 129
Fort Ellsworth (Kans.), 101
Fort Gibson (Okla.), 9 n.9
Fort Hays (Kans.), 131
Fort Larned (Kans.), 4, 91, 92, 97 n.2,
    101, 105, 106, 107
Fort Leavenworth (Kans.), 64, 65, 66,
    71, 72, 75, 91, 97, 98, 99, 100,
    101, 102, 105
    as beginning of Santa Fe Trail, 3
Fort Lyon (Colo.), 4, 70, 91, 94, 98,
    99, 101, 105
Fort Mackay (Kans.), 26
Fort Mann (Fort Atkinson, Kans.), 11
Fort (or Camp) Nichols (Okla.), 4,
    81 n.12, 100 n.8
Fort Osage (Mo.), 52
Fort Riley (Kans.), 101
Fort Scott (Kans.), 72
Fort Sill (Indian Terr.), 87
Fort Union (N. Mex.), 4, 11, 37, 38,
    39, 40 n.4, 42–43, 49, 51, 65, 66,
    69, 70, 71, 85, 90, 91, 94, 95,
    96, 97 n.2, 98, 99, 100, 102

Fort Zarah (Kans.), 106, 107, 109, 111, 112
 plan of, 113
Fouglin, John, 13, 14
Franke, Fritz, 76, 107, 110, 112, 116
Franke, Mrs. (Ernestine Huning's mother), 76, 107, 110, 112, 116
Franklin, Mo., 1, 64
Franz, E. D., 79 n.9
Franz, Mrs. E. D., 79
freight wagons. *See* wagons and wagon trains
Frenger, Mr., 77
Fugate, James M., 4
 adventures of, 29–36
 his fights with Indians, 29–34, 35–36
 at Pawnee Rock, 34
Funke, Mr., 77

Galisteo, N.Mex., 124
Gallinas River, 102
Garrard, Louis Hector, 64, 65
Gazette (N.Mex. newspaper), 12
geese, 22, 23
Gettysburg, Battle of, 72, 75
Glorieta, N.Mex., 124
Glorieta campaign, 96
Glorieta Pass, 124 n.8
gold
 discovered in Colorado, 52, 73
 panning for, 61–62
 discovered in California, 73
Golden, N.Mex., 124
Gonzales, Nesario, 122, 124, 125, 127, 128, 131, 132
government wagon trains. *See* wagons and wagon trains
Grasshopper (now Valley Falls), Kans., 66
Gray, James S., 70 n.9
Gray's Mill (or Gray's Ranch), 70, 94
Great Bend, Kans., 131
Great Bend of Arkansas River, 23, 28, 43, 68, 91, 108
Greenhorn Creek, 104
Green River, 6
Gregg, Josiah, 8, 126, 135
Gregg, Kate L., 3
guaje (gourd for drinking water), 125
guajete (container made of hide), 123
Gurulé, José Librado Aron, 120
 recollections of, 122–33
 and Indian woman, 128–29
 in Kansas City, 129–30
 works on railroad, 131
 buys wool suit in Kansas City, 133
Gurulé, Nicolás, 122

Hancock, Maj. Gen. Winfield Scott, 106, 107
Hathaway, John L., 110
Hathaway, Mary E., 110
Hathaway, Ralph, v, 110, 111
hay, for military animals, 99, 100, 101
Hayes, Seth, 38, 41, 42
Hays City, Kans., 131
Heart of the New Kansas, The (Smyth), 28
Henderson, Mr. (wagonmaster), 66, 68, 71
Hole-in-the-Prairie (Kans.), 55
Hot Springs (Las Vegas, N.Mex.), 82
"how," Indians' use of, 60
Hoyt, Dr. Henry F., 121
Huerfano River, 62 n.14, 99, 104
Hughes, John T., 68 n.4
Hulbert, Archer Butler, 3
Huning, Ernestine Franke, 108
 picture of, 76
 massacre of her mother and brother, 76, 106
 diary of, 77–83
Huning, Franz
 tintype of, 74
 visits Germany, 75, 79 n.9
 and massacre at Plum Buttes, 106–8, 111, 112–16
hunting, on the Santa Fe Trail
 of prairie chickens, 21
 of buffalo, 22–23, 24, 53, 55, 56, 69
 of ducks, geese, turkeys, 22, 63
 of prairie dogs, 46, 55
 of antelope, deer, elk, 48, 49, 69
 of rabbits, 69
Hurricane Bill, 118
Hutchinson, Kans., 30 n.2

Independence, Mo., 15 n.11, 18, 20, 28, 40, 51
 Courthouse Square, picture of, 2
 Alvarez arrives at, 10
 courthouse of, 28
 Brake leaves, 39

Indian Mound (Chouteau's Mound), 35 n.5
Indians, 20, 62
hostile, and attacks by, 4, 9, 12, 17, 30, 68, 75, 84, 87, 90, 91, 92, 96, 98, 107, 112, 113, 114, 115, 126, 127, 128, 131
dances of, 21
scalping by, 21, 35
in Kansas, 29
Fugate's fights with, 29–34, 35–36
kill livestock, 31, 35
steal livestock, 32, 81, 100
kill Spaniards, 35
like sugar, 44, 46, 59, 60, 128
like crackers, 44, 46
look for food, supplies, 44–45, 59
give war whoops, 45
described, 60
villages of, described, 60–61
friendly, 79
steal gold, 81
protection against, 101
Christy on, 111, 116
confederated tribes' war on government, 112
get rations at Fort Dodge, 129
See also Apaches; Arapahos; Caws (Kaws); Cheyennes; Comanches; Jicarillas; Kaws (Caws); Kiowas; Mescalero Apaches; Navajos; Osages; Pawnees; Plains; Pueblos; Shawnees, Wyandottes
Iron Spring, 70

Jarvis Creek, 68 n.6, 91
Jicarillas, 20
Jim's (or Jimmy's) Camp, 62 n.16
Jones, John S. (J. W.), 31 n.3
Jornada, the (in southwestern Kansas), 12, 15, 47, 71, 75, 80 n.10
Junction City, Kans., 107

Kansas, 52
major part of Santa Fe Trail in, 2, 3
Indians in, 29
Kansas City, Mo., 40, 52, 53, 61, 65, 75, 98, 122, 124, 129, 131, 133
as starting point of the Santa Fe Trail, 3
Negro band in, 130
Kansas Pacific Railroad, 131

Kansas (Kaw) River, 66, 68, 78, 101
Kaws (Caws), 21, 55, 78
Kellogg, David, 52
diary of, 52 n.2, 53–63
sees comet, 55
hunts buffalo, 56, 57–58
encounters rattlesnake, 56
describes Indian, 60
Kickapoo Rangers, 54
Kidder, Homer H., 108, 109
Kiowas, 38, 44, 46, 59, 68, 117
and massacre at Plum Buttes, 108
fight at Little Cow Creek, 118–19
Know Nothings (American Political party), 57 n.8
Kozlowski, Martin, 102 n.10
Kozlowski's Ranch, 102
Kronig, William, 82 n.17
Kronig's Ranch, 103

Lamar, Colo., 61 n.12
Lane, William Carr, 11, 12, 13
Las Animas, Colo., 61 n.13
Las Placitas, N.Mex., 120, 121, 122, 123, 124, 130, 132, 133
Las Vegas, N.Mex., 4, 76, 82, 97 n.2, 102, 124, 125
Lawrence, Kans., 53, 54, 72, 101
Leadville, Colo., 85
Leavenworth, Kans., 52, 77, 84, 85, 88
Lemita, N.Mex., 126 n.11
Lexington, Mo., 28
Lincoln, Abraham, 66
Little Arkansas Crossing, 9, 107
Little Arkansas River, 22, 24, 68, 101, 117
Little Colorado (Colorado Chiquito, or Cimarron), 103
Little Cow Creek, 116
Little Turkey Creek, 55, 79
livestock, 89, 90, 124, 125, 126, 127, 129
protection of, in blizzards, 18, 59
killed by Indians, 31, 35
corralling of, during Indian attacks, 32, 34, 87, 92
stolen by Indians, 32
feeding of, 69
breaking of oxen to yoke, 85–86, 94
Mexican, 93

stampede of, 93–94
  at Fort Lyon, 99
"Log Island," 13
Long's Peak, 70
Los Estados (Kansas City), 122, 133
Lost Creek, 8
Lost Spring, 55, 107
Louis, Mr., 77, 80
Lummis, Charles F., 7

McCamish, Kans., 54
McCoy, William, 15 n.11
McDaniel, Capt. John, 68
McDougal, George, 62
McFerran, Maj. John Courts
  as quartermaster, 96–97
  his trips on the Santa Fe Trail, 98
  report by, 98–102
  journal of, 102–5
McGee, William, 110
McNees Creek, 99
Magoffin, Susan, 64, 65, 73
mail service on the Santa Fe Trail, 12,
  69
Majors, Alexander, 32 n.4
Majors and Russell, 32 n.4, 33
Mansfield, 'Squire, 42
manta (coarse white cotton suit), 123,
  130
Martin, Bird, 57
Matthewson, William ("Buffalo Bill"),
  117n.17
  fights Kiowas at Little Cow Creek,
  118–19
  Kiowas dub him Sympah Zilvah—the
  Strong Man, 119
Maxwell, Lucien B., 103 n.11
Maxwell Land Grant, 70
Maxwell's Ranch, 95, 103
Meigs, Q.M. Gen. Montogomery C.,
  96, 97
Meketa, Jacqueline, 37 n.1
Mesa, Cañon and Pueblo (Lummis), 7
Mescalero Apaches, 18
  See also Apaches
Mexican War, 12, 15, 68, 73, 96
Mexico, 6, 80
  gains independence, 1, 6
  won't recognize Alvarez, 7
  trade with, 15
  traders from, 93

Middle Spring (near Elkhart, Kans.),
  126
Miranda, Guadalupe, 9
missionaries on the Santa Fe Trail, 73
Mississippi Yawger (gun), 89
Missouri, 13, 15, 73
  gains statehood, 1
  Santa Fe Trail in, 1
Missouri Intelligencer, 1
Missouri Stage Company, 70 n.8
Montaño, José, 132
Mora River, 103
Mormon emigrant route, 75
Morris, Kans., 41
Mountain Branch of the Santa Fe Trail,
  25, 39, 97 n.2, 126 n.10
Muddy Creek, 67
mules, 38, 40, 79, 89, 112, 113, 114,
  115, 125, 126, 129
  in storm, 21
  protection of, in snow, 26
  Brake drives, 46, 48
  stolen, 78
mule skinners, 121

Navajos, 20, 122 n.5
Negro soldiers and women, 131
New Mexico, 13, 15, 18, 29, 31, 41,
  64, 73, 81, 122
  Santa Fe Trail in, 2
  and expedition from Texas, 7
  Alvarez's report on, 8–10
  trade with, 28
  Brake takes job in, 37
  Department of, 96
New Mexico Federal Writers' Project,
  120
nuns, on the Santa Fe Trail, 73

Ocaté Creek (or River), 99, 103
Oklahoma
  Santa Fe Trail in, 2
  Panhandle of, 15, 81, 100 n.8
110 Mile Creek, 52, 53, 55
On Two Continents (Brake), 39 n.2
Oregon Trail, 73–74
Osages, 22, 23
Otero, Seller and Company, 4
Ozawkie (Osawke), Kans., 67

Palo Alto, Battle of, 96
Pate, Capt. Henry Clay, 54, 55

Pawnee Fork, 35, 47, 101
Pawnee Rock, 58, 110
  picture of, 33
Pawnees, 9, 58
Pecos Pueblo, 16 n.13, 102 n.10
Pecos River, 20, 102
Perea, José Leandro (or Leander), 121,
  122, 123, 124, 125, 127, 128,
  130, 131, 132
Perkins, B. F., 42
Pigeon's Ranch, Battle of, 96
Pike's Peak, 45, 70
Plains (Indians), 128 n.14
Plum Buttes, 106
  massacre at, 76, 108–10, 112–16
  described, 108
  relics found at, 111
Point of Rocks, 51, 81 n.14
Poñil River, 103
"popper" (whip cracker), 88
Pottawatomie Creek, massacre at, 54
prairie chickens (grouse), 21, 55, 61
prairie dogs, 46, 47, 48, 55, 127
"prairie schooners," 91
Price, John, 55
proslavery men, 54
Pueblo, Colo., 53, 62 nn.14 and 15,
  104
Pueblos (Indians), 25
punche ("tobacco"), 123
Purgatoire River, 70, 94, 99, 104

Quantrill, William Clarke, 72
quicksand, 24, 43

Rabbit Ear Creek, 49, 99
Rabbit Ears Range, 81
rabbits, 69
railroads, 4, 131
Raton Mountains, 70, 98, 103
Raton Pass (N.Mex.), 4, 53, 70, 85,
  94, 103 n.12
Raton Route, 70, 98, 99, 100, 103,
  104, 105
rattlesnakes
  Vanderwalker on, 4, 88
  Kellogg encounters, 56
Rayado, N.Mex., 103
Resaca de la Palma, Battle of, 96
Richmirs (?), John, 10
Rio Grande, 121, 122 n.5, 124
Rio Grande Valley, 125

Rio Napeste (or Napestle), Spanish
  name for Arkansas River, 129 n.15
Rittenhouse, Jack D., 85
Road to Santa Fe, The (K. Gregg), 3
Robidoux, Antoine, 14
Rogers, Mr., 53
Romero (Roma), Mr., 112 n.12, 113,
  114, 115
Romero, Esquipulo, 122, 123, 128,
  130, 131
Round Mound, 81 n.14
  picture of, 50
Russell, Majors and Waddell (com-
  pany), 32, 33, 85, 94
Russell, William H., 15 n.12, 31 n.3,
  32 n.4

St. Louis, Mo., 13, 37, 39, 75, 77,
  78, 82, 97, 107
Salt Creek Valley, 67
San Carlos River, 104
Sand Creek, 80, 99
  massacre at, 116 n.16
Sandia Mountains, 120
sandstorms, 47, 50
Sanford, Colonel, 42
San José, N.Mex., 102
San Miguel, N.Mex., 16
San Pedro Mountains, 124
San Pedro Viejo (pueblo), 124
Santa Clara Springs, 82 n.16
Santa Clara valley, 82
Santa Fe, N.Mex., 3, 5, 29, 31, 36,
  39, 45, 55, 64, 76, 98, 102, 105
  picture of plaza at end of Santa Fe
    Trail, ii
  capital of Spain's province of New
    Mexico, 1
  trade with, 1–2, 9, 15, 29, 68 n.6
  Alvarez in, 6
  Confederate troops occupy, 70
Santa Fe Gazette, 12
Santa Fe Trail
  history, romance of, 2, 64, 110
  trade on, 2, 3, 73, 80, 122 n.5, 125,
    129
  middle years of, 3
  freight wagons on, 4, 15 n.12, 16,
    26, 31, 65, 66, 70, 84, 97
  demise of, 5
  storms on, 7, 8, 9, 12, 13, 14, 15,
    16, 18, 21, 22, 23, 24, 25, 26–27,
    47, 59, 77, 79, 81

mail service on, 12, 69
proposed refuges for travelers on, 12, 13
Connelly's trips on, 15 n.9
Sumner and First Dragoons on, 16 n.14
picture of wagon train on, 34
women on, 64, 65, 73–74, 131
after the Civil War, 96
patroling of, 97 n.2
old, 101, 105
wheel ruts of, near Chase, Kans., 110
soldiers as escorts on, 112
Sapello River, 102
Satanta (Kiowa chief), 68
scalp dance, 21
scalping, 21, 35
"Scouting Adventures" (Fugate), 28–29
Scranton, Kans., 53 n.4
Sedgwick, Gen. John, 99 n.7
serapes, 123
Shawnees, 21
Sherman, Pat, 70
"Shot-Mouth Charlie," 87
Sibley, George C., 3
Sierra Grande, 81
Sloan (later Russell), Marian, 64
Smith, Henry
  recollections by, 65–72
  described, 66
  enters University of Michigan, 72
Smith, Red Head, 57
Smoky Hill River, 101
Smoky Hill Route, 52, 106
Smyth, Bernard Bryan, 28
snow, melted for water, 25
snowstorms. See storms on the Santa Fe Trail
Soldier Creek, 67
South, Seneca, 9
Southwest on the Turquoise Trail (Hulbert), 3
Spain, 6
Spaniards, killed by Indians, 35, 36
Spanish Peaks, 61, 70
Speyers, Albert
  encounters snowstorm, 14, 26
  identified, 15 n.9
Steck, Michael
  picture of, 19
  as agent for Apaches, 19
  as superintendent of Indian Affairs for New Mexico Territory, 19
  resigns as superintendent, 20
  as gold miner and investor, 20
  returns to Hughesville, Pa., 20
  dies in Winchester, Va., 20
  trail letter by, 20–27
Stewart Stemens Company, 84, 88, 91
storms on the Santa Fe Trail
  blizzards and snowstorms, 7, 8, 9, 12, 13, 14, 15, 16, 18, 21, 22, 23, 24, 25, 26–27, 47
  protection of livestock during, 18, 26, 59
  mules in, 21
  sandstorms, 47
  thunderstorms, 77, 79, 81
Sumner, Lt. Col. Edwin Vose, 16 n.14
Sweet Water Creek, 103

Taos, N.Mex., 130 n.16
Taos Lightning (liquor—"Mule Skinners' Delight"), 90
Taylor, Sarah ("Aunt Sally"), 41 n.5
Tecolote, N.Mex., 102
Tecumseh, Kans., 53
Tejón, N.Mex., 124
Tejón Cañon, 124
tewas (leather moccasins), 123 n.6
Texas, expedition from, to New Mexico, 7, 70
Timpas River, 98
Tomasito, 130 n.16
Topeka, Kans., 53, 65, 67, 68, 70, 71, 78, 101
trading
  with Santa Fe, 1–2, 9, 15
  on the Santa Fe Trail, 2, 3, 73
  in wool, 80, 122 n.5, 125, 129
travois, of Plains Indians, 128
Trinidad, Colo., 70, 94, 104
Trujillo, Joaquin, 122
Turkey Creek, 8, 55, 68, 91
  See also Little Turkey Creek
turkeys, 22, 23, 63

United States Army, 12, 101, 107, 112, 131
Upper Cimarron (Casa Depallo, or Flag Spring) Spring, 80, 81 n.11, 100

Upper Semer. *See* Upper Cimarron
    Spring
Utes (or Utahs), 20, 49, 61, 62

Valley Falls (Grasshopper), Kans., 66
Vanderwalker, George E., 84, 103
    on rattlesnakes, 4, 88
    reminiscences of, 85–95
    picture of, 86
Vermejo River, 103
Vicksburg, Miss., 72

Waddell, William B., 32 n.4
Wagon Mound, 49, 82 n.16
wagons and wagon trains, 84, 114, 121
    of army and government, 4, 15 n.12,
        16, 26, 31, 65, 66, 70, 92, 97
    pictures of, 34, 54, 67, 112, 124
    form corral, 69
    and wool trade, 80
    Vanderwalker describes, 89
    formation of, when attacked, 91–92
    Mexican, 93
    of merchants, 100
    contents of, on return trip, 130
Wah-to-yah and the Taos Trail (Gar-
    rard), 64
Waldo, David, 15 n.11
Waldo, McCoy and Company, 15

Walnut Creek, 22, 30 n.2, 57, 91, 101,
    106 n.1, 108, 111
war whoops, 45
Watson's Ranch, 103
Webster, Daniel, 8
Westport, Mo., 28, 40, 54, 55, 68
Wet Stone Basin, 51
Wet Stone Spring, 81
Whetstone Creek, 81 n.14, 99
whiskey, used to treat cholera, 132
Willow Bar (Okla.), 15
Wilmington, Kans., 78
Wilson, Levi, 66
Winchester, Jim, 56
Winchester, Kans., 67
wolves, 55
    hunt buffalo, 24
    steal Brake's boot and bridle, 38, 49
women, on the Santa Fe Trail, 64, 65,
    73–74, 131
Woodruff, Dr., 58 n.10
wool trade on the Santa Fe Trail, 80,
    122 n.5, 124, 125, 129
Wootton, Richens ("Uncle Dick"),
    70 n.9
    his toll road to Raton Summit, 70,
        95, 103
Wyandottes, 40

Yellow Woman, 116 n.16